THE EMOTIONALLY HEALTHY YOU

©2025 Vicarium, LLC

drkarthikramanan.com
Phoenix, Arizona
Send feedback via the website.

ISBN: 979-8-9926559-1-9

Published with the assistance of Blaze Experts
Editing by Jeffri-Lynn Campbell
Cover and Interior Design, Text Design, and Composition by Mandy Love

THE EMOTIONALLY HEALTHY YOU.

Dr. Karthik Ramanan

CONTENTS

CHAPTER 1   **FOR GROWTH SEEKERS ONLY**   1
Who Are You Becoming?

CHAPTER 2   **THE FIVE PILLARS OF EMOTIONAL HEALTH**   14
Powerful Behavioral and Lifestyle Factors

CHAPTER 3   **BELIEFS**   23
The Lens Through Which We See the World

CHAPTER 4   **BEHAVIORS**   36
Our Truths Determine Our Reality

CHAPTER 5   **HABITS**   44
How Do Your Habits Serve You?

CHAPTER 6   **EXPECTATIONS VERSUS STANDARDS**   53
The Framework for Joy

CHAPTER 7   **BOUNDARIES MADE BETTER**   62
What You Tolerate Continues

CHAPTER 8   **PERFECTIONISM, IMPOSTER SYNDROME, AND SELF-CRITICISM**   71
How You Measure Up Depends On What You Measure

CHAPTER 9   **SELF-CARE**   82
An Easier Way to Support Ourselves

CHAPTER 10   **A NEW PERSPECTIVE**   93
How to Practice Emotionally Healthy Communication

CHAPTER 11   **THE FIVE PILLARS OF EMOTIONAL HEALTH**   107
The Five Pillars in Practice

CHAPTER 12   **THE EMOTIONALLY HEALTHY YOU**   125
24 Principles for an Emotionally Healthy Life

APPENDIX   **CITATIONS AND STUDIES**   132
Sources and Resources

ACKNOWLEDGEMENTS   136

CHAPTER ONE

For Growth Seekers Only

Who are you becoming?

This book is specifically for those of you who are stressed out at work, want more personal time, or have a desire to quit your job and pursue your dream. It is for the entrepreneur who pursues a meaningful business idea or the life of a creator who is running into the wall of burnout. It is for the successful professional and business owner who achieves more and more, only to find something missing deep inside. It is for those of us who deeply desire that sense of purpose we seek in this world.

I wrote this for you, the growth seeker who is tired of protecting your past and wants to move forward into a future that represents the best version of yourself. Welcome to the community!

These tools and strategies help to create optimal everyday mental health. It will help you silence that critical voice in your head to get out of your own way and live a purposeful life. It's not necessarily something you can use to process the past; it is an emotionally healthy way to move forward. You will learn to appreciate the moments you face challenges or obstacles, as you will handle them with more emotional resilience and appropriate emotional intensity, and your duration of sitting in the struggle will shorten. You will come away with an understanding of what you can control and a whole-body approach to regulating your emotions. It will even help you understand what isn't being said and respond appropriately in your meaningful relationships.

I want you to come away with a toolbox of skills you can apply to cope, navigate, and thrive!

I designed this book to help you realize you are not broken! You have simply adapted to living a certain way, and now you can live on purpose by learning to process situations and regulate your emotions properly. Here, I will teach you to own the gifts from your own story and recognize how the pain that caused things you may dislike about yourself has also had a positive impact. Focus on that reality because pain reveals our superpowers! I want you to know it's okay to take your professional life personally, so we'll get personal to improve your professional life.

My Story

Imagine standing right at the edge of the room, looking through a large window that envelops your peripheral vision. You gaze outwards through the window from 500 feet in the sky, not a building around you to obscure your view of the New Jersey horizon. From this vantage point, you can see the gorgeous sunsets, the magnificent weather patterns, and the nighttime view of thousands of small lights scattered across the urban landscape. You feel you are standing on top of the world!

That's exactly where I was in my late 20s. I vividly remember one night when I reflected deeply on the sacrifice it took to get there. In 2005, I graduated from Cornell University and began working at one of the world's premier investment banks. I was honored, excited, and ready to put forth every ounce of will and energy within me to learn and grow in the company. Little did I know of the oncoming Great Recession! Despite watching longstanding banks crumble and losing friends to layoffs, I responded the only way I knew how: Work harder. Come in earlier. Wake up at 2:00 AM to send an email, then go back to bed waiting for the 4:00 AM alarm. Work a bare minimum of 12 hours at the office. Work from home. Come in on weekends and holidays. Say "yes" to everyone at all costs. I was determined to make myself indispensable.

My efforts were noticed and rewarded. And here I was, years later, living in my own apartment, alone, for the first time. I felt tremendously blessed. I paid off my undergraduate student loans. I paid off my parents' credit card debt. I gave more to charity than I ever thought I could at that age. And I was a single guy in New York! All that hard work had paid off.

Well, that part was true if you judged only from the outside. The truth that nobody knew? I hated the man in the mirror.

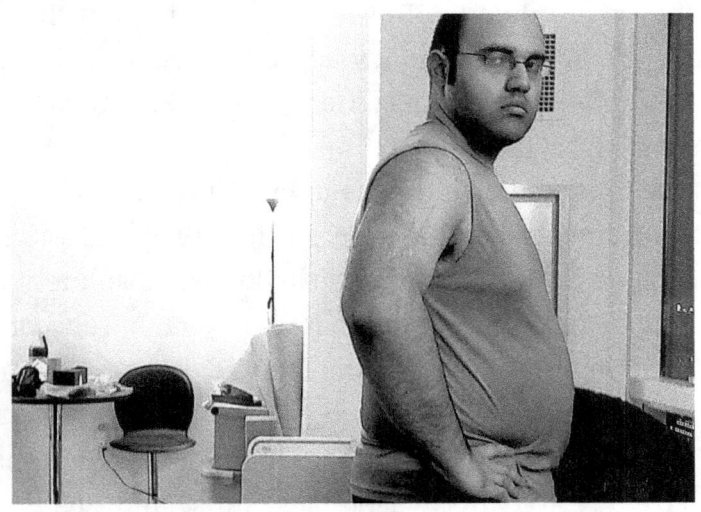

Every morning, I'd wake up and look at my severely overweight body, sagging eyes, and depleted vitality before amping up and asking myself how I was going to make it through the day without letting anyone know how much I was struggling inside. More importantly, how was I ever going to find the one missing thing in my life that I so desperately wanted: a deep, meaningful relationship and, eventually, a fulfilling marriage?

Work harder! Of course! That was the answer to everything.

I was too ashamed to consistently go to the gym for fear of being judged for not knowing what I was doing. So when I discovered some intense 90-day and 60-day workout programs that my friends had great success with, I knew I had found the answer! I had initial success, along with diet changes, but eventually, just as with all other weight loss attempts, I plateaued and eventually gave up.

I hit rock bottom. Although I didn't realize it at the time, it was actually a beautiful place.

When life is going well, we typically don't take chances. We don't risk what we have, as underwhelming and sometimes undesirable as it may be, to seek something greater. The known is safer than the unknown. But at rock bottom, that flies out the window. We are willing to try anything. We are willing to say "yes" to the things we otherwise would reject. At rock bottom, we have nothing to lose.

As the universe would have it, I saw my sister after a three-month window, and in that time, she lost 30 pounds! Her chronic cystic acne had vanished, and she looked absolutely vibrant. I had to have this, too! Scared to my soul and barely containing my excitement, I asked her what she did, knowing I was going to follow the exact same protocol.

"I've been eating a raw, whole food, plant-based diet," she revealed. "Fresh fruits, vegetables, nuts, and seeds, just as they're found in nature." As crazy as that sounded then, I had to give it a shot.

But it wasn't just the food that was different. I had always been a "cold turkey" type of person when it came to making change. I was a full-speed-or-nothing perfectionist who inherently believed that if I can't do it perfectly, it's not worth doing at all.

My best ideas in life had carried me to that moment, but what if I did everything the exact opposite? What if I transitioned into a new, intuitive way of eating to see where this would take me? I was determined to relinquish expectations and avoid daily scale weigh-ins for "accountability," and that was a lot easier said than done for my former self!

Three weeks after embarking on this endeavor and choosing to eat 100% the way my sister had taught me, my clothes fit better, and I felt better. I had to see what the scale said! I looked down that morning, and there it was. I beheld a number lower than any weight I had ever seen as an adult! I felt a surge through my body; a light radiated through me! It was almost as if I had been wearing sunglasses my whole life, and now they were off in an instant, and I could see the world in more vibrant colors.

What if the body I wanted, the confidence I wanted, the relationship I wanted, and even the life I wanted were possible? What if the health, marriage, and meaningful life that I had written off for myself was within my grasp after all? What if the only thing holding me back was...me?

❚❚ What if the only thing holding me back was...me?

I was on my way to losing 100 pounds, and I let life's momentum take me. I never went anywhere without my homemade, intense green juices and as they noticed the weight loss unfolding, coworkers, friends, and even my mother approached me for advice on getting healthier. I gave them recipes, occasionally brought delicious, healthy food with me to share, and these people lost weight. I witnessed type 2 diabetes go away, chronic migraines disappear, and high cholesterol levels fall back to normal after years. Hypertension was gone and chronic joint pain vanished to the point that people were getting their lives back!

I'll never forget Mother's Day 2012 when my mother came to New Jersey to visit me.

For years, my mother worked extremely hard, not just at home taking care of her family, but also at her high-stress corporate engineering job. When I would go to visit my parents, I'd take my mother to the grocery store and she would request I drop her off at the front door before parking the car to save her a few extra steps of painful walking as she struggled with her weight and experienced joint pain in her knees and ankles.

Inspired by the weight loss of her two kids, she asked me for help. I bought her a juicer, gave her some recipes, and she gradually implemented the same strategies my sister and I used.

And here we were on that memorable Mother's Day. My mother had lost 80 pounds! The same person who struggled to walk without pain was now walking up and down the Hudson River with me on that beautiful day...for 15 miles! At the top of our route, we took a break for a picnic lunch. My mother looked at me and said, "Thank you, Karthik. You've given me a healthy life I didn't know I had left."

This was fulfilling! And this was the moment I knew I had to make a career change. I had to figure out how to make health and wellness my new professional life path.

I left my Wall Street career and enrolled in Southwest College of Naturopathic Medicine (now Sonoran University of Health Sciences). I started living as the ideal version of this "Dr. K" that I was building for the future instead of existing as a reflection of my past.

While loving myself for the first time, I attracted the love of my life. I met Samantha in medical school, and we got married soon after. That life I had wanted, craved for years, and questioned whether I deserved became a reality.

The truth is, we change only when it hurts enough. And once it hurt enough for me, I was open to possibilities. I generated the passion to change my lifestyle, and despite my work routines, I made it happen.

In my lifelong efforts to chase joy, I missed out on the wonder of the life we're already born into. Just because we're struggling doesn't mean we're failing.

❝ Just because we're struggling doesn't mean we're failing.

Our struggles and pain direct us toward the life we want if we're willing to make the choices and take the actions needed to get there. I changed the way I ate and started losing weight. I exercised. I slept better. And the best part was, I recognized that being a perfectionist and prescribing to the "never good enough" philosophy of achievement was not the only way to live at a high level.

Albert Einstein once said, "We cannot solve a problem with the same mind that created it." If we try to solve a problem while inside it, using the same means that led us there, we cannot truly solve it. Rather, we must look outside the situation at hand to observe and think more clearly.

We need a completely different approach to achievement,

one that includes well-being, to maximize ALL the important aspects of life: health, relationships, and our work.

When we take care of ourselves first, we make things happen. At work. At home. Everywhere. We are the force multiplier in our lives. We are the vehicle that drives our mission and purpose in everything. With a focus on becoming emotionally healthy, the overwhelm diminishes. When the time is right, we escape from the life that isn't serving us and move into a life of purpose. For me, that was becoming Dr. K., making a difference in people's lives, and fulfilling my dream of being a published author.

Who do your circumstances stop you from becoming?
Work can be overwhelming. I get it. You feel like you have to be at this job or in this career because it pays the bills, and how else is your family going to make it? Or maybe you feel stuck while owning and running your business and can't find the freedom you wanted to achieve through the business in the first place. Here's the truth, Friend. If you didn't have that work, you would find a way to make ends meet. Maybe you'd find a different path that feeds your soul or a different way to take care of your family. We are all built with an innate desire to survive, and you would find a way!

We feel overwhelmed because our expectations are higher than our reality. Unless we are extremely clear with ourselves as to what those expectations are, we're going to feel frustrated and overwhelmed. What if you made more realistic expectations for your job? What if you came to grips with your current reality and decided to craft a new reality with flexible work arrangements, a more engaging and exciting role, or something else you need to change so you can work full-time on your dream business or create the life you envision instead? What if you accepted the fact that your business created a new job for you, one where you feel you can't step away from the machine to enjoy your personal life because without you, the business would fail? You must begin by processing your emotions, even if you're a highly rational person like me.

When we're overwhelmed by running a business or diligently working on our careers, we aren't grounded in the structures of our brains that handle rational thought. We are exposed to stimuli that trigger the emotional centers in our brain. So the first thing to do is process what's going on there when we're in a more relaxed, clear-headed state.

What are your fears? Write down all the fears you associate with your job. Is it your boss? Are you worried about the project you're working on, or a client? Are you concerned whether your bonus will come through, or if you're not being paid enough? Are you afraid the business you built, inherited, or bought will fail? Write down all of the fears associated with your work life.

You can download this worksheet or the entire workbook at my website, drkarthikramanan.com, and you can access all the resources you will find in this book on my dedicated Reader Resources page.

Now go do something you enjoy for 15 minutes or a half hour. Consider being physically active so you feel good in your body. Then, go back and read your list of fears. What comes up for you?

Unprocessed fears wreak havoc when you're operating at work. And when you get home, those fears drain the energy that would allow you to work on your passion projects during your free time.

Next, write down on another sheet of paper (or your workbook page) the worst thing that could happen if you made some balance in your life. What kind of balance do you want? What if you worked out a flexible work arrangement with your manager so you could work remotely? What if you dedicated yourself to a morning routine like a trip to the gym or writing in the Dr. K Journal, which you can find as a download on my website? What is the worst that could happen at work if you decided to prioritize yourself and your mental health just a little bit more?

Do the same thing if you run your own business. What's the worst that could happen if you prioritize your mental health just a little more?

Let's say solving your overwhelm from work was simple. Write down possible solutions. What would the solution look like? Now that you've taken fear and emotions out of the picture, you're just looking at rational decisions here.

Now that you have a logical frame of reference around what your work means to you and how it impacts your life and could be different, what does it look like to prioritize your personal life as an ambitious individual?

What about work-life balance?
Be honest. When you're with your significant other or kids, how often do you have your phone nearby? If you're trying to rest and take care of yourself, how often are you thinking about the next thing you have to do for work? All you're doing is fooling yourself into thinking you're spending personal time.

I hate to break it to you, but there's no such thing as work-life balance. Real life doesn't support living in perfect harmony, putting your work behind you for the day, and spending time with your family. It's an idealized state that does not exist.

If you're ambitious in your professional life and have any amount of desire to spend time with your family or in self-care, the assumption that you can find perfect balance and harmony between the two is unrealistic.

So, what's the answer? Consider this: As human beings, we have an incredible ability to remember past events and imagine events that have yet to occur. We think time has three parts: past, present, and future. The truth is the past and future don't exist. All there is is right now!

❝❝ All there is is right now!

Let me prove it to you. Humans are extraordinary communicators in the animal kingdom in large part because we have organized language. Close your eyes and pull up a memory in your mind, but don't use any language to describe it to yourself. Refrain from using words that describe color, shapes, locations, or time. Go ahead and try it! It's extremely difficult, if not impossible, because we can't fully experience a memory without language. There is no past or future; there's just our ability to describe it with language.

What does this have to do with prioritizing your personal life? Remember, there's no such thing as work-life balance, and there's no past or future without language. I'll say it again: All that exists is right now.

Be intentional with your present moment. Concentrate on being where your feet are in the moments you are with your family and in the moments you are focused on your own well-being. And yes, be present in the moments you are "in the zone" at work.

Everything you do, do it on purpose.
If you're with your family, put your phone away. If you're taking personal time, be intentional and take that time without allowing yourself to feel that self-imposed guilt for what you think you should be doing. (Don't worry, I'll show you how to do

this later on in this book). Focus instead on the warmth of that cup of tea, the feeling of the sunshine on your face, the smell of the candle burning beside you. Perhaps you can't balance your work and life, but you can absolutely maximize the reward of the time you do have with your family and with yourself. Be here and now.

Here's the answer, my friend. Leave your phone out of your bedroom so you don't look at it when you wake up. Take some time every morning to set your intentions for the day. Meditate for a few minutes to clear your mind before you ever touch your phone. Journal to solidify your plan, and visualize yourself executing that plan and spending quality personal time. Then, take on the day!

We all have two nonrenewable resources: Time and Attention. Once we spend our time or give away our attention, we cannot get it back.

Samantha and I weren't even a month into our marriage when she expressed her displeasure with our personal time together. I was working 12-plus hours a day and weekends to learn how to get the Dr. K Show and my business up and running, and when I was spending time with her, I kept feeling agitated that I had more to do. When we talked about how this wasn't working, I remembered something my father taught me when I was a kid. I was trying to do homework while watching TV, and he said, "You can't do multiple things at once. Focus on one thing at a time, then do the next." That memory helped me learn to prioritize my personal life while growing my business.

If you want to have a fulfilling personal life and live an ambitious professional life, you must become the master of your attention. Focus your attention with intention, and you will live a full, extraordinary life.

Do yourself a favor. Stop focusing on what isn't working. Focus instead on your desired outcome. What is your WHY? What do you want your life to mean? Focus on that goal, and allow your working life today to be a means of funding that dream. If you want it badly enough, you WILL make it happen.

This book will help you stop living as a reflection of your past and start leaning into your vision of a future of vibrant health, pleasurable relationships, and the immense purpose that you truly desire.

I believe in your greatness.

~Dr. K

CHAPTER TWO

The 5 Pillars of Emotional Health
Powerful behavioral and lifestyle factors

Which words immediately come to mind when you think about the term "physical health?" Is it diet? Exercise? Wellness?

Now, what comes to mind when you read the words, "mental health?" Do you think of anxiety? Depression? Bipolar? How come when we say "mental health," the first things that often come to mind are mental illnesses?

What's the difference between mental health and mental illness, anyway?

According to the American Psychiatric Association, mental illnesses are "health conditions involving changes in emotion, thinking or behavior (or a combination of these). Mental illnesses are associated with distress and/or problems functioning in social, work, or family activities."

"Mental illness refers collectively to all diagnosable mental disorders - health conditions involving significant changes in thinking, emotion and/or behavior, distress and/or problems functioning in social, work or family activities."

When they say "diagnosable," they're referring to the Diagnostic and Statistical Manual of Psychiatric Disorders or the DSM-5. This manual clearly outlines the various criteria required to be able to diagnose a patient with conditions like generalized anxiety disorder.

I don't like the term "mental disorder." It implies something is wrong with a person. Language is powerful. The words we use to describe what we're experiencing matter, not just explicitly, but also the implicit meanings that come with the use of specific language. We all have different degrees and different flavors of challenges, and just because someone doesn't qualify for a mental disorder diagnosis per the DSM-5 doesn't mean they don't have mental health challenges to address. And when someone is diagnosed, it doesn't mean something is deeply wrong with them.

They go on to say that "mental health involves effective functioning in daily activities resulting in productive activity (work, school, caregiving) and healthy relationships." It is the ability to adapt to change and cope with adversity.

Does that mean mental health is purely the absence of mental illness? To me, no. True mental health is about resilience, fulfillment, joy, and vulnerability. It's the ability to handle emotional storms, acknowledge them for what they are, and allow them to pass without wreaking havoc on your personal, social, or professional functions. Mental health is the ability to use your mind as a tool rather than allowing it to use you. Mental health is emotional health. Balanced health.

> **❝ Mental health is the ability to use your mind as a tool rather than allowing it to use you. Mental health is emotional health. Balanced health.**

To address mental health challenges, we generally have two avenues today: counseling and psychiatry. Both are incredibly powerful when individualized to a person's needs. When a person finds the right therapist for them and the right therapy, magic happens. I personally benefited immensely from EMDR therapy years ago, and it sent me on my current trajectory. I believe everyone can benefit from working with a great counselor, both when we're struggling and when we're feeling good. When we take the psychiatry approach, especially in some acute situations, we can experience desperately needed relief, and certain conditions necessitate the use of appropriate medications.

Yet, there is still more that goes into our emotional well-being. If you remember from earlier, my personal journey to emotional health came through nutrition.

As I was navigating my weight loss journey, watching friends' and colleagues' symptoms of type 2 diabetes, hypertension, chronic joint pain, and chronic migraines reduce or disappear, a thought crossed my mind. Do we have a headache because of the lack of ibuprofen in our system? Or do we have a headache as a result of the conditions we're in, such as mild dehydration?

What if many of the challenges we're dealing with result from our being intricately adapted to survive in nature, not in this crazy modern world we now find ourselves in?

Imagine an ordinary house plant. Some of its leaves are wilted. It leans awkwardly to one side. Its colors are no longer as vibrant, and the soil appears dry and cracked. This plant is not doing well. How might we go about solving this problem? Think for a moment what you might do to help this plant.

Did you think about giving it water? Maybe it isn't getting enough sunlight, or perhaps the soil needs to be changed.

Notice how you didn't start with "let's give it a pill." Your first thought wasn't, "Maybe I just got a defective plant. Maybe it's broken."

Even those of us who have never successfully kept a houseplant alive know that we first address the water, sun, and soil factors. Why? Because those are the fundamental determinants that this organism needs to survive.

What if we applied the same concept to ourselves with the five powerful behavioral and lifestyle factors that I call the Five Pillars of Emotional Health?

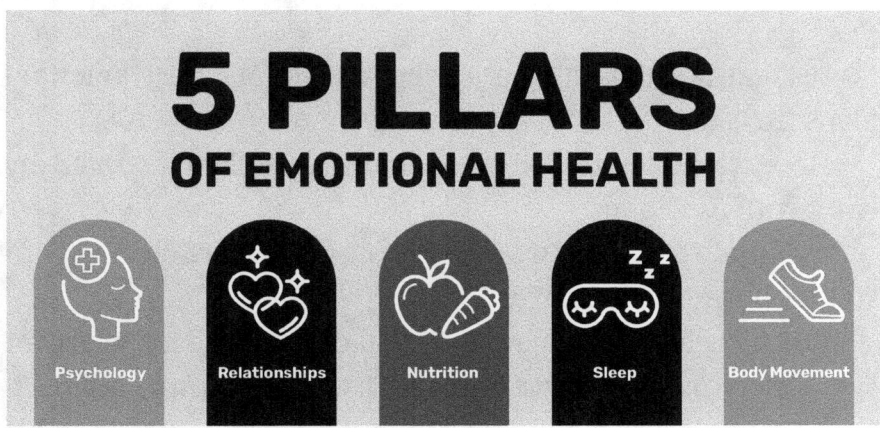

What IS emotional health?

Emotional health is a person's ability to identify, process, and act upon feelings in specific circumstances and over time.

What does that mean? What makes up emotional health? How does emotional health differ from mental health? And how does one go about building strong emotional health?

Emotional health incorporates emotional intelligence and emotional resilience. Let's unpack those two concepts.

1. **Emotional intelligence** is the awareness of one's emotional state and those of others, especially in response to external stimuli. Have you ever been around someone who, especially in the face of immediate adversity, simply knows how to carry themselves and how to interact with others? This is an example of emotional intelligence, which is an extremely important aspect of leadership at all levels.

2. The other part of **emotional health** is emotional resilience. This is one's ability to adjust to circumstances and recover from emotional setbacks. How well do you respond to bad news? Do setbacks and acute stress send you down a dark road? How quickly can you return to your fully functioning state of mind?

Just like health is not merely the absence of illness, emotional health is not the act of suppressing emotion.

Here's an example of emotional health demonstrated by two fictitious friends:

Jack and Susan are two small business owners dealing with similar business challenges.

Jack is a high-achieving individual experiencing stagnant company growth. When his costs rose significantly, his business started to lose money each month. Determined to keep his team members employed, he cut out as many other expenses as possible and reduced his own pay to make ends meet, but the financial stress impacted his family life and eventually, his marriage began to come undone. Through all this, Jack refused to let anyone know. When it all started, he felt great shame and anxiety but never shared with anyone that he was in pain. As the weeks went on and the isolation continued, his stress increased to the point that he took naps during the day, felt no energy to do things he loved, and generally stayed in a pessimistic state of mind. The positive work environment he spent years constructing started to fade, and he began to wonder if he was about to lose his family, as well.

Jack is a proud man trying to tough it out, suffering in silence. Unfortunately, our character Jack is emotionally unhealthy.

Susan, on the other hand, also felt anxiety through difficult times. Susan is a high-achieving entrepreneur, spending years and countless dollars building a small business she loves. As costs rose, she, too, had to make impossible decisions. Rather than making them while she was feeling low or high, Susan was willing to experience those emotions and let them pass. She recognized that she needed to allow herself to grieve the changing state of the world and her struggles in business. She knew these circumstances could take a toll on her marriage, and she was open with her partner, asking for the support she needed personally to be able to navigate the challenging time. Once she processed and re-centered herself, she could focus on taking care of herself so she could figure out how to make her business thrive again. This pivot allowed her to continue driving the impact she desired while supporting her team members to make her vision a reality.

Susan is emotionally healthy.

How do you create unshakeable emotional health?

1 **Your psychology.** This is the study of your mind. It is the lens through which you see the world. It includes established thought patterns and beliefs, the way you talk to yourself, your history of trauma, and the stories about "facts of life" you grew up around. This is personal development. It's a willingness to step outside of your comfort zone and discover what patterns have been running your life, honing your ability to create and live into a vision of the person you wish to be.

2 **Your relationships.** If you've studied personal development, you know we are the average of the five people and ideas we spend the most time with. It bears repeating because it is so monumentally important. If our relationships are sour with those five people we spend the most time with, our emotional health will suffer significantly. There's no way around it.

Working on your relationships means addressing the pain points with your significant other and those close to you. It means having conversations with your boss or your coworkers to create an environment that's most conducive to emotional intelligence and emotional resilience. It's releasing who you think you should be and embracing who you are so you can attract the best people into your life. Become a Growth Seeker and surround yourself with as many Growth Seekers as you can!

3 Your nutrition. What does nutrition have to do with emotional health? A lot! I think you'll agree that if our brain and nerve function isn't operating at proper capacity, we're not going to feel well. And if we don't feel well, our emotional resilience suffers.

Neurotransmitters are compounds that aid in sending signals through our nervous system. Examples include epinephrine, dopamine, serotonin, GABA, and many others. What you may not know is that 90% of the neurotransmitters in our body come from the gut. An estimated 100 trillion bacteria in our gut are responsible for neurotransmitter production as well as many other functions it seems we learn about daily. What I'm talking about is called the gut microbiota, and their genetic material is called the "gut microbiome." These bacteria provide us with essential compounds needed for optimal function, and we provide them with a place to live. However, the types of bacteria that grow in our gut depend upon what we eat.

If we eat too many foods that harm our gut microbes, we'll lose out on the necessary amounts of the vital short-chain fatty acids and other compounds that those microbes provide. Eventually, that leads to less-than-optimal function in organ systems that require those compounds. Diets high in refined sugars, fried fats, processed foods, and animal products tend to produce a sub-optimal gut microbiome, whereas diets high in whole plant foods and soluble fiber are essential for a thriving gut microbiome and, therefore, optimal emotional health. You must eat well to feel well.

4 Your sleep. Let's be honest: we high achievers like to sacrifice sleep to get more done, don't we? A major project at work? Stay up late. Building your company?

Get up early. I get it because I was that way, too. During my undergraduate studies at Cornell University, I routinely slept four hours a night, and in 30 weeks over two semesters in my freshman year, I pulled 37 all-nighters. During my years on Wall Street in my 20s, I got more sleep. Six hours, yay! I'd work late, stay up late, be on call while constantly checking emails, and then get up early to get to work the next day. I prided myself on needing as little sleep as possible.

After four years of medical school, that lifetime of sacrificing sleep caught up to me in the form of various hormone imbalances and burnout. It took a toll on my emotional resilience, which, as you now know, is a component of emotional health. It wasn't until I shed my workaholic identity as a badge of honor that I took my emotional health to the next level. We can work hard and work smart...while still getting our critical sleep.

Our brains process the day's happenings during sleep. It's when we place the day's events and lessons into long-term memory and form connections in our brains. It's also the time when our bodies detoxify and shed waste. Sacrificing sleep WILL catch up to you eventually, and if you want to build emotional health while ending or avoiding burnout, prioritizing sleep is a non-negotiable.

5 **Your exercise.** Motion drives emotion. How energized do you feel after a workout? Endorphins run high, your blood flows and your body and mind feel in sync. Working out isn't as much about weight loss as it is about training our bodies to operate at the highest level. If you want to feel your best, there is no substitute for moving your body. Emotional health requires physical health!

Understanding the physical activities that make us feel alive and help us navigate our emotions is another way to feel more connected to ourselves and less reactive to situations around us.

My point is this: Whatever challenge you're facing, you're not broken. There is always hope. Your emotional health is about living into the ideal version of yourself. You will when you apply the five pillars of emotional health. Consider your psychology, your relationships, your nutrition, your sleep, and your exercise. Which of these five do you need to work on?

It's also important to remember that even when we implement all the strategies and improve our five pillars of emotional health, we're still going to make mistakes because we're human beings. Our minds and bodies were designed to keep us safe in nature, and we're asking them to do things they weren't designed to do.

CHAPTER THREE

Beliefs

The lens through which we see the world

To understand anything about the life we're living and the world around us, we must first understand how we got here. To do that, we need to understand the circumstances in which our bodies and minds were developed and defined. We're taking the long way to understand how we became who we are, so buckle up and let's go!

We were built for nature, with every cell, tissue, organ, and system in our bodies designed to survive. We were not built for this modern world we've created for ourselves. I'm not saying we should all go back to living in the forest, as I would be the first to swat at the mosquitoes, but if we can incorporate some fundamentals of nature back into our everyday lives, we'll be better off. After all, when we're not feeling great, we rarely feel worse when we venture outside, and more than likely, being out in the sun and fresh air helps us feel better.

There's a big difference between surviving and thriving. If we can't survive the threats of nature, thriving doesn't matter, so first and foremost, our bodies and minds are tuned for survival. We could even argue that we weren't designed to live in growth and fulfillment as human beings since we were built for survival.

Everything in nature assumes that energy is scarce. While a meal we cook at home or eat at a restaurant may have an abundance of calories without much effort, we must work to obtain all those calories in nature. If we were out in nature and had to acquire food for ourselves, finding and gathering fruits and vegetables or taking down an animal, obtaining those calories would take immense energy, so our bodies were designed to conserve as much energy as possible. Today's acts of driving to your local grocery store or ordering delivery take far less energy to get food! So when we assume energy is scarce, we must also look at the human body and its functions in terms of how this helps us in nature. When we do that, our behaviors make more sense.

Think of all the organs in your body. Visualize your heart, which has been pumping without rest since before you were born. Think about your diaphragm sitting below your lungs, expanding and contracting, mostly without your focus or attention. Picture your digestive system meticulously churning all the food you eat. And think of the exertion of your skeletal muscles every time you move and exercise.

Despite all those busy organs and systems, the brain utilizes more energy than any other organ in the human body. It burns about 20% of its calorie intake just to operate at baseline: processing sensory information, directing essential motor functions, and regulating autonomic functions like breathing and heart rate. It takes even more energy to problem-solve or apply our minds to something new.

Our survival instincts inherently dictate that we do not exhaust that energy whenever possible. Change becomes progressively more difficult after a certain point in life, so becoming "set in our ways" is not a defect. Have you ever wondered why people rarely change their musical or food tastes over time? It's actually in line with how we're designed.

We conserve mental energy by chunking data, systematizing processes, and creating procedural memory. Think about the first time you learned to drive a car. You probably gripped the steering wheel tightly, nervously bouncing your eyes between the speedometer, rearview mirror, and side mirrors while trying to remember where you were supposed to go. Fast forward to today, and imagine driving home from work or taking another route you drive often. Have you ever "zoned out" and awakened to realize you're almost home? Did you really zone out? Not at all. You were still taking in all the sensory information. You might not have consciously told yourself, "Green light, ok, I can keep going," but you processed that sensory information through a series of rules you constructed in your mind over the years and continued to drive forward. Isn't driving far less exhausting now than when you first started?

By contrast, have you also noticed how tiresome it can be to drive to a new place with lots of traffic, pedestrians, or construction? When I drive to a new place with my wife and try to figure out the directions towards the end of the journey, especially in congested areas, I often ask her to turn down her music. "Ah, yes, turn down the music so I can see," she jokes. But it does help!

Our brains save energy by churning information based on recurring stimuli and repeated actions through an "autopilot" function called the Default Mode Network. The processes we often repeat take less energy now, but when circumstances change, our inherent actions still drain our energy.

Why does the human mind thrive on routine?

The physiological functions of routine and habit allow us to commit more things to procedural memory and use less energy.

When we create habits and routines, we commit more actions to procedural memory. Consider our earlier driving example. When we begin learning something that takes a lot of energy, we sometimes feel it in the form of exhaustion. You learn something new: a new skill or lesson, and you can feel tired afterward because you've used energy. But then, later in life, the action feels easier if you've done it hundreds or thousands of times. When we chunk sequences of thoughts and actions together, they become more routine.

So why do we thrive on routine to save energy? Here's a life example. I lived in an apartment complex with a friend of mine during medical school, and we decided that I would get the prime bedroom, and he would get the dedicated covered parking spot for our apartment. (In Arizona summers, a covered parking spot is priceless!) That meant my car would be parked in any uncovered spot, wherever I could find one open that day. Every morning, when I would leave, I'd have to remember where I parked the night before. It would break me out of a thought I was having and even take me a few extra seconds when I needed to look for my car. When we moved a couple of years later, I got to park my car in the same spot every day. After a few days, my mornings felt marginally less rushed. Then it hit me! I hadn't entirely understood the drain of the extra effort it took to stop and think about the location of my car every day at the old apartment. It might not seem like much, but the energy drain adds up when these events pile up.

Before we could buy our first home together, my wife and I rented for a few years. We never felt like the place was truly ours, so we didn't make all the adjustments and customizations to make it feel like home, but given my affinity for tech, I had a few Philips Hue colored lights in my home office that I could automate and set to a variety of scenes. My wife would just smile and shake her head. "Is it really that hard to turn on the light switch?" In isolation, no. She had a point, but when we purchased our first home, I outfitted it with more Philips Hue products. One of my new automations turned on all the lights

26

inside and outside the house 30 minutes before sunset. When it was time to go to sleep, we commanded Siri, and the lights switched off while forest sounds began to play in our bedroom to create a restful environment.

About a month in, my wife says, "Okay, I have to admit it's pretty awesome having the lights automated. Just not having to think about flipping them on and off in each room every day, it adds up!"

Routine allows us to get into a flow and a rhythm without having to think about things. Setting up our environment to take some of that activity off our plate or create a simple flow in our routines saves valuable brain energy.

Routine serves us when we can create one that gives us an emotionally healthy foundation. Our world is busy enough! Creating a few routines and crafting our environment to reduce our thought load can significantly improve our emotional health.

How We Got Here

As babies, we have very few skills and instincts. We know how to cry, and we know how to suckle. Then we develop our senses, quickly prioritizing smells, sounds, and sights and understanding, "This is mother, this is father, this is safe." Then we start exploring, walking, and stumbling. We begin to play peek-a-boo, thinking that they can't see us if we can't see them. Soon after, somewhere between two and three years old, we recognize that the world around us is separate from ourselves.

When I was four years old, I would play with my dinner for hours. My mother had spent a long day in graduate school classes and working on her research, and the last thing she probably wanted to do was watch me not eat for two hours every night. She tried the kind approach for over an hour, finally uttering sternly, "Karthik, eat your dinner!"

I would immediately finish my food. Looking back, I think I basked in having my mother's attention during those two hours, and I enjoyed that as a kid. But somewhere before I turned five, I realized my mother was sad when I didn't eat my food, and I didn't want that, so I consistently ate my dinner without hesitation. Why did that happen seemingly overnight?

Around 5 to 7 years old, we start to recognize and further develop the idea that we have an effect on the people around us. From there, we begin chunking data, detecting patterns, and assigning meaning. We create stories that become our truth later on in life. We establish the ground rules for who we are and who we are not. In many cases, these truths come from the child version of ourselves, whose mind was simply trying to make sense of the world around us with the machinery we had at the time.

How does this lead to how we see the world today?
There are beliefs. "I believe things will get better soon," or "I believe I can set a personal record at the gym today."

Then there are truths. These are the rules by which we live, the framework and lens through which we see the world. Truths go beyond believing; we simply "know."

What forms our truths? It's never a simple answer, for the classic question of nature versus nurture complicates it. If we look at the grand scheme of our genetics, the code is very similar, gene-wise, from one person to another. We find more variation in epigenetics, where the genes turned on and off can transmit through two to three generations. There are theories about how our genes turn on and off because, as humans, we experience cultural beliefs passed through growing up in certain cultures with certain people. More than those things, however, our childhood experiences influence the beliefs we bring into adulthood.

My Truth Cycle

The Truth Cycle is a simplified model for understanding how we functionally handle our day-to-day lives. Neuroscience is much more intricate and complex; however, complexity doesn't have to be complicated, so this model helps us understand how we operate today.

Please refer to the diagram here as I explain the model. My video on the Truth Cycle is also available in the book resources section of my website at drkarthikramanan.com/reader-resources

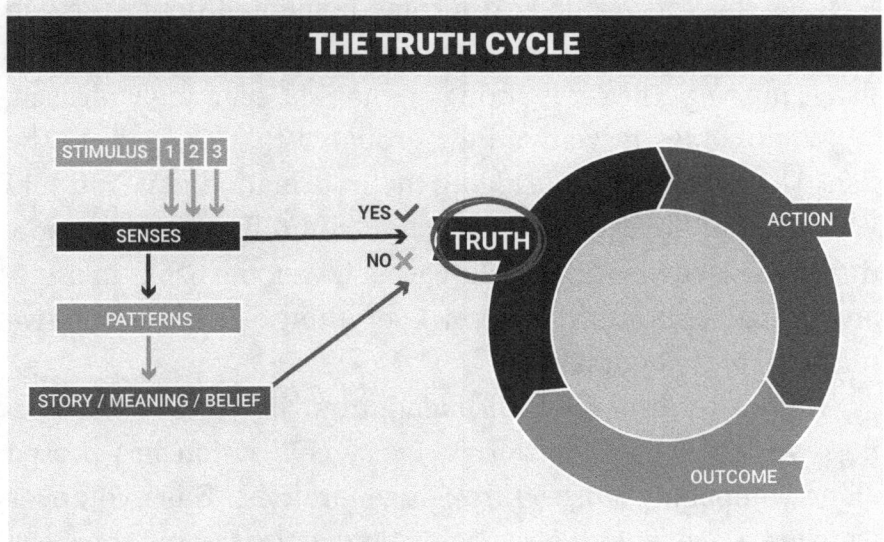

A stimulus is an outside factor that creates a behavioral or physical response within us. It can be the sight of a car, the sound of the wind, or the smell of your favorite soup. It can also be a collection of events, like the sound of your phone ringing and the caller ID that appears visually.

When our senses perceive stimuli from the outside world, the signals travel through the appropriate neurons to our brain, and we interpret them. Eventually, we begin detecting patterns in our senses. Other animals share this trait, too. If you have a dog at home, you may notice how they have figured out which days are work days and which are not. They see the patterns in how we get up, move around, and prepare for the day. They detect patterns from the sensory inputs, so they know what comes next in the pattern, and they're sad before we even leave the house.

The next step sets human beings apart. We can't limit our perspective to only look at senses and patterns. If two independent events in our brain seem associated, we instinctively create a bridge between them.

Take this for example. You come home and notice the fish bowl has been tipped over. The carpet below it is wet, and the fish is missing. The cat is sitting on the sofa, seemingly pleased.

What comes to your mind? Probably that the cat ate the fish! That's your mind bridging the information gap. You told yourself that the cat ate the fish, but truthfully, you only know that the fish bowl is tipped, the carpet is wet, the fish is missing, and the cat is sitting on the sofa. Everything else is the story we instinctively tell ourselves.

This pattern happens throughout our lives. As human beings, we are wired for stories. Every civilization has passed along compelling stories through generations. Have you ever watched a movie with great actors and actresses, but the story didn't hold up? How much do we enjoy those, even with accomplished acting? Stories are vital for the human mind.

The more we see a story, the more we create meaning, a lesson, and a moral from that story. And the more we apply that meaning, the more it becomes a belief. We convince ourselves based on what we've seen and experienced numerous times.

One of the common foundational beliefs that I experienced myself and have worked on with many clients is the foundational belief that "I'm not good enough." It may be even more specific, like, "I'm not smart enough," "I'm not good-looking enough," "I'm not resourceful enough," or "I'm not kind enough." It can sound like "I don't stand up for myself enough" or "I'm not capable enough." It always comes down to the feeling of not being good enough, which often translates to the sense that "I'm not enough."

It's a foundational belief because patterns occurred when we were younger, and we assigned meaning based on whatever we could assume or create then. Our minds at that time were not as advanced as those we developed as adults; however, we've evolved on those same belief patterns that we began with, some of which may be true and some not.

However, at a certain point, the meaning moves from believing to simply knowing. We treat it as the truth—there is no room for negotiation.

Once this happens, as new stimuli arise and we engage our senses and detect patterns, we examine this new data against our truths to save energy. Does it check out? Okay, carry on. Does it not fit the truth? Reject it.

It's easier to reinforce our truths than to question them. This is why it's so difficult for people to embrace new ideas, evolve musical tastes, or order anything other than the standard menu items at a handful of go-to restaurants.

Truth is a powerful force because it drives our conscious and unconscious actions. We will take actions that are consistent with our truths, so debunk your untrue beliefs as they were formed under circumstances that occurred when you assigned meaning to them. That's all! If that meaning is not empowering, you can change it now as an adult because you can reprocess those memories. You can reprocess the past, invite new meanings for new beliefs, and reinforce those that empower you.

Consider these examples:
"I am a good person!" It's difficult to consider doing a friend wrong.

"I am a people pleaser." We'll find ways to bend and accommodate others' needs to feel we're getting their approval.

"I'm a workaholic." It will be hard for this professional or entrepreneur to put away the computer and relax. (I get it. I've been there!)

The actions we take drive the outcomes we receive in life. If we eat poorly, we get poor health outcomes. If we don't work hard, we might not get promoted. And eventually, those outcomes reinforce the truths we hold.

Have you ever wondered why most of us fail repeatedly at New Year's resolutions? "New year, new me! I'm going to go on this diet and work out every day at the gym!" By January 5th, the party is over. Why? Because we started making the changes at the level of actions, but those actions weren't consistent with our truths. Maybe one truth is, "I always fail at New Year's resolutions," or "I'm not worthy of being healthy and loved." The moment we use up our willpower to diet and go to the gym, the moment we run into any resistance, we quit. The old outcomes continue, and we can tell ourselves, "Yup, it happened again." And around and around we go.

The only way to create new outcomes in our lives is to understand the truths we currently hold and where they came from. These truths are the lens through which we see the world. Reframing this lens allows us to lean into our superpowers and become our ideal selves.

The truths we have developed about ourselves and the

world around us dictate our reality. And I hate to break it to you, but this reality you're living in is subjective. Each person has their own subjective reality. So what is objective reality, then? That would be laws of nature or the construct of the universe: things we don't even fully understand. But our day-to-day life is driven by our subjective reality. Since our subjective realities differ, two people can experience the same situation and come away with two completely different stories of what happened.

Additionally, since our subjective realities differ, we might feel strong imposter syndrome in our work life despite everyone around us telling us how great we are at that very thing that feels crippling on the inside. Our subjective reality is not theirs. These truths, these subjective realities, are powerful. They lead to actions that are most consistent with our truths about ourselves and our world.

Actions, naturally, lead to results. Typically, results correlate with the quality and quantity of our actions, so we can expect results to reinforce our truths. If you struggle to believe in yourself because you hold a disempowering truth about yourself, taking different actions to create new results is challenging. How do we break out of this? Creating new, empowering truths about yourself is the key to experiencing a better life. When you replace your old, disempowering beliefs with new, empowering truths, new actions naturally follow and ultimately create new outcomes in your life.

❙❙ Creating new, empowering truths about yourself is key to experiencing a better life.

Did you know that the parts of the brain used for memory are the same ones that light up on brain scans while we use our imagination? We can all agree that the memories of our past affect how we act today. With this fact of neuroscience, we can create powerful imagination through visualization to create new "memories" of our future. This picture of what's to come influences a new belief, creating new actions that drive different results.

Here is a process I've used with clients who struggle to envision changing their lifestyle habits, improving their relationships, or even being kind to themselves. It's the same technique I used to go from lacking self-confidence and living in a cloud of shame to the person writing this book today.

You can do this by yourself. Spend 5 to 10 minutes daily in a quiet place, visualizing yourself in your ideal future. Focus on your emotions and what you feel in your body. Focus on the sensual elements of this new reality: the sights, the sounds, the relationships. You want to internalize the experience fully. Going through a guided visualization is sometimes easier and more effective when you have someone's voice guide you through the prompts so you can allow your mind to wander and experience rather than think about what you should think about next.

When done regularly and intensely, you will create the same powerful neural pathways created by memories, and as a result, you'll start to take new actions, get new results, and reinforce a new belief in yourself.

You deserve to feel and be your best! Access my 7-day guided visualization program, "Believe in Your Greatness," on the Reader Resource Page at drkarthikramanan.com. It may help you overcome self-doubt and build lasting confidence, generate momentum in your life, and establish healthy emotional health habits.

Sometimes, it's hard to imagine we can do things we've never done before, but our imagination and memories are neurologically similar processes. Visualize the future you want and the person you want to be. Then, live into that vision. Experience that future state as you meditate and powerfully internalize that vision. Your imagination will now serve as a blueprint for the confident, vibrant, healthy person you wish to be.

Self-confidence isn't something reserved for other people! Faith in yourself isn't some magic gene you are born with. You can develop it. Look at the things you've overcome in your life. Give yourself a moment to reflect and appreciate what you've been through and overcame. It's substantial! If you've survived all those challenges and are still here, what does that say about you? You are powerful!

You, too, can shed self-doubt, build true confidence, and establish emotionally healthy habits because you deserve to live a life of purpose.

CHAPTER FOUR

Behaviors

Unconscious or conscious, our truths determine our reality

In prior chapters, I've discussed how we developed the lens through which we see the world. How does this lens affect our behavior? In summary, we take conscious and unconscious actions consistent with our beliefs (and developed truths) of ourselves and the world around us.

How to identify your unconscious behaviors

Sigmund Freud classified three levels of consciousness: the conscious mind, the preconscious mind (what we now know as the subconscious), and the unconscious mind. Understanding these three levels is essential to defining unconscious habits.

The distinction between subconscious and unconscious is not always clear, and the terms are often used interchangeably, even by professionals, so let's clarify that.

The conscious mind is what you think about, hear, and see. You are aware of these things: thoughts, memories, and things that come to mind quickly. The conscious mind cannot process too many things in parallel, but the subconscious mind (the preconscious mind) constantly scans.

Think again about driving. You may be thinking consciously about where you're supposed to go. You're checking the GPS, your speed, and maybe listening to a podcast or music, but your subconscious mind is continuously scanning for red lights and threats because we don't react to those things consciously. We see that red light, and we instinctively stop.

When you dig into the unconscious mind, the level below the subconscious, you find the pool of deeply held thoughts, feelings, and belief systems. It's also where repressed memories and resulting behavior stem from. Our behavior pattern urges emerge in ways we can't understand—they may manifest as anxiety or panic, but they could just be behavior patterns we've never consciously noticed.

It's also important to consider the underlying design of our minds and bodies. Remember, we were made for nature and designed for survival. Our intricate machinery, including the levels of consciousness, was made for a world in which we no longer live. While some of our habits may be inexplicable at times, looking at them through the lens of being made for survival in nature may provide clarity and perhaps even self-compassion.

How do we identify our unconscious habits? It is challenging to use the conscious mind to investigate the unconscious, so the route I find the most effective is to observe the behavior, or more specifically, tune into areas of our conduct.

One way is to identify how we spend our time. We've all had that experience of, "Oh, I have a lot to do." Maybe we have a project coming up for work or a paper that's due for school. We have things we need to do, but what do we do instead? We might play games on our phones or clean the house. Whatever it is, the distraction causes us to procrastinate, right? In the end, we want to look at that behavior. How do we spend that time?

When you examine how you spend your time, you can determine what is truly important to you. Go beyond the conscious mind into the subconscious and unconscious mind, and you will find your unconscious priority. For instance, playing a game on your phone or scrolling social media may not be a priority for you, but the escape it provides is essential.

Here's an example. Maybe you are putting off that project for work or your business. You know it needs to be done. It's stressing you out that it's not complete. Yet scrolling social media is what you instinctively do when you know you could be working on that project. When you look inward, you may feel inadequate around the project and tell yourself, "I don't think I can do this!" But the deadline looms. And like almost all of us in school or at work, when the deadline approaches, our focus becomes superhuman, and we get the job done. Why couldn't we have done this earlier rather than distracting ourselves? It's not that scrolling the feed is important to us; it's the avoidance of that pain that matters. We don't want to face the project that brings about feelings of imposter syndrome, so we avoid it until we can procrastinate no longer.

So, identify your unconscious habits by observing how you spend your time—without judgment. Just observe and take note.

Another way is to look at the language we use. Words are powerful. They mean specific things to us, so the language we use inside our minds and out loud is important. Generally, we agree with each other in terms of language because we understand what certain words mean and don't mean, with some variance. Nonetheless, words are powerful.

Let's take an example. Say you made a mistake on that work project and reacted in one of two ways.

One is, "Oh, I'm such an idiot." The other is, "Oh, I made a mistake."

Which one is more damaging than the other? Take a moment and think about it.

"I am an idiot" is much more damaging. Why? Because it is a statement of identity. When we make a statement of who we are, we believe it in our subconscious and unconscious minds. At an unconscious level, we will take action consistent with our truth about our identity. When we say, "I am an idiot," we make "idiot" an aspect of our identity. And it's not even a belief; we're treating it as the truth! So what happens going forward? We find ourselves in more positions where we can reinforce that (untrue) truth.

By contrast, if we say, "Oh, I made a mistake," there's no statement of identity. Yes, "mistake" is still a subjective judgment call. But we're separating who we are from what we did. It only means we did not execute or plan the way we wanted. Reframing provides an opportunity to learn and grow because there's no judgment associated with our identity. It's simply, "I made a mistake. I want to learn from this going forward."

We always want to be cautious of the language we use, not just out loud, but in the words we say to ourselves. If you catch yourself saying something disempowering to yourself in your mind, the first step is just to notice it. It's okay that you said it. Now you've seen it, which is the first and, in my opinion, the most challenging step to producing lasting change that allows us to live at our highest, most emotionally healthy level.

We can change things in our unconscious mind once they become conscious, so let's bring our beliefs and our values into our consciousness with an exercise. You can download the worksheet at my website, drkarthikramanan.com, or take out a sheet of paper and write down "I am..." on one side and "I am not..." on the other.

Take 10-15 minutes and turn off any distractions in your space. Put your phone away. Take out your pen, and just let it do the thinking. There's no need to edit your thoughts here.

When you list words after "I am" and "I am not," focus on words you'd use to describe yourself. If you choose a word that entails a role (ex: "I am a mother"), explain how you feel about yourself in that role (ex: "I am a good mother").

Continue to write down the words that come to your mind, no matter what they are. They may look like, "I am an idiot." "I am incapable." "I am not good enough." "I am not smart enough." Or they may look like, "I am kind." "I am loyal." "I am too loyal." "I am right."

List whatever comes to mind. These are your truths, your lens through which you see the world. Some of them might be helpful, whereas some of them may not be.

How do our truths influence our behaviors? How do we change that?

Think of your truths as mere lessons. They are shortcuts our brain has created over the course of our lifetime to utilize less energy. It's a survival mechanism, so every piece of data that we receive is collected for speed processing and coping.

Remember driving? We collect data through vision and sound as we drive. We recognize and store street sign names and which lane we're in, all while filtering through shortcuts, patterns, and existing beliefs. So when somebody cuts you off in traffic, is your first inkling or gut reaction one of anger or fear? Do you immediately think, "What is wrong with that person?"

What if that person was on their way to the hospital and they had somebody needing attention in their car? Is that the first thing that comes to mind? Not usually. Often, the first thing that comes to mind is, "What a jerk!" because that's the original shortcut.

Once we realize our patterns are shortcuts, we can say, "Okay, is this serving me, or is this not serving me?"

Sometimes, they serve you! Many shortcuts you have learned help you. If, for example, you have a shortcut for changing lanes to exit the highway, you use the right-turn blinker, check your blind spot and rearview mirror, and make the turn without thinking about it, it just happens! That shortcut serves you, but if one of your truths is, "I'm not good enough," that shortcut leads you to the feeling that you're not worthy, which doesn't serve you.

We can begin the work of changing our truths only when we realize that every thought pattern, behavior, and reaction to somebody else's words has been filtered through them.

The first step in changing those subjective truths is understanding what they are and where they came from. We must realize that it's not about judging the circumstances, situations, people, or upbringing that led us to this truth. No, it's an objective look at the fact that it happened. Therefore, this happened, and then this is how I adapted. Ask yourself, "Is this helping me anymore?"

How to separate belief (fantasy, imagination, idea, the abstract, fiction, dream, theory, our "truth") from reality
Our truths determine our reality by affecting the things that are largely unconscious to us. But the other thing that affects our reality is where our attention focuses, and that's a conscious decision.

If you want to change your day-to-day relationship with the world around you, you must accept that your truths affect your unconscious relation to the world around you, while your attention affects your conscious interaction with the world around you. Those two things, our truths and our attention, determine our subjective reality.

> **❠❠ Two things, our truth and attention, determine our subjective reality.**

If you decide to change (you don't want to be the same way any longer) and you can unwind your assigned meanings without deep intervention for trauma and the like, then you continue forward and say, "These are my subjective truths, and this is where they came from. They are my truths, not necessarily the truth."

This acceptance is simply an acknowledgment of what happened. It's not a judgment. It doesn't condone the event, the pattern, or the situation. It's not saying it's okay. It's just saying, "It happened," and the meaning you apply to what happened can be changed!

I look back at periods of my life when I struggled with self-criticism and had difficulty believing in myself, and I think about the profound emotional challenges that came from that. It was a level of pain I would not wish upon anybody, and I certainly would not want to go back in time and relive those days. I also wouldn't change a thing because those challenges allowed me to do what I do today. Living in the depths of the darkness of my mind enabled me to understand somebody else at a deep level today.

Now, look back at your list. Ask yourself what situations in your life may have led you to believe this way. Think of both the empowering and disempowering things on your "I am" and "I am not" list and ask yourself, "Why?"

Keep going deeper. Look at which situations earlier in life led you to your strongest truths today, both the empowering and disempowering ones. You may realize that some situations that led you to those disempowering subjective truths are the same circumstances that created your superpowers! What did your pain allow you to do that you would not have been able to do otherwise? When you live in that possibility, you can look back at those truths and say, "Okay, I'm changing this one. It doesn't serve me anymore."

Who do you want to be? Who is the person that you want to become? Who is the ideal version of yourself? In that ideal, what do you stand for? What is the type of life that you live? What do you want your life to mean? And what is the legacy you leave for the people around you?

Map out that person! How do they think? Schedule their day. Think about their habits or routines. How do they do things? Make a list and begin doing each of those things, as that is how we change our beliefs to influence our behaviors and live in the vision of our ideal self!

You can live in a reflection of your past, or you can move into the vision of your ideal self. The choice is yours.

CHAPTER FIVE

Habits

Constructive or Destructive:
How Do Your Habits Serve You?

We talk about habits all the time. We say, "Oh, it's just a bad habit. I'm trying to be good." As we learned in chapter four on behaviors, language is essential, so let's examine it closely.

"It's just a bad habit." So far, so good!

"I'm trying to be good." Let's look at the word "trying." Hold a pen in front of you. Now, I want you to try to drop it. Did you drop it? I said try, not drop. Is it still in your hand? Then you didn't drop it. Where does "try" come into play here? It doesn't. How else do we typically use "try?" What if you ask your friend to join your other friends for a night out, and your friend says, "Oh, thanks for the invite! I will try to make it." What's already going through your head? We often use "try" to give ourselves a way out, so I suggest following Yoda's advice: There is no "try." Either we do, or we do not. We set our intentions, we take our actions, and that's it!

Back to "I'm trying to be good." If we continue this bad habit of drinking sugary beverages, does that make us not good? Are we a bad person? Using this type of language is not helpful because we already judge ourselves when we use the whole concept of good versus bad habits.

"Good" and "bad" are inherently subjective terms. We use those words for many things in life, and all those connotations get integrated when we say "good habit" or "bad habit."

It's a subjective reality to judge a habit as good or bad. I much prefer "constructive" and "destructive" instead.

How do we determine a constructive habit versus a destructive one?

I have a habit of putting things on credit cards. To some, purchasing with credit cards feels like a destructive habit because they don't pay the balance, accrue interest, and build additional credit card debt. But what about the person who charges things to their credit cards, pays them off immediately, and then reaps all cashback rewards or redemptions for travel? The action itself is the same: purchasing with a credit card. The judgment we place upon it, attaching "good" or "bad," is based on our point of view created by past experiences and the things we've learned.

If we take that perspective, there's no such thing as a good habit or a bad habit. They're just habits! Some might be constructive towards the person we want to become. Some may be destructive as they relate to the person we want to become. That's it.

If you have ever tried to train a dog to sit, stay, lie down, or look at you, you're training a habit for your dog. Is that a good habit or a bad habit? It doesn't matter! It's a habit.

How are habits created?

Four components create habits: a cue, a craving, a response, and a reward. The cue is a sensory trigger, such as what you see, hear, smell, taste, or touch. The craving is the feeling generated and the origin of all our actions, the desire. That emotional craving is the genesis of every action we take. That craving leads to the response, that action we take or don't take.

The reward is the payoff resulting from the action. The reward is vital to creating the habit cycle because the original cue is not reinforced without the payoff. When the payoff occurs, we release dopamine in response to the cue, building anticipation and craving. And so the cycle continues.

So it's the cue, the craving, the response, and the reward. The more the cycle occurs, the more habitual and procedural the action, and the stronger the habit cycle becomes. The judgment we place on that habit is up to us.

Imagine a cookie sitting on the countertop of your kitchen every single day. You see the cookie. You want the cookie. You eat the cookie, and the cookie tastes good. Then, every time there's a new cookie the next day, it's reinforced. So, is that a good habit or a bad habit? You might say that eating a cookie a day is probably not a good thing, but if you replace the cookie with an apple, it's "an apple a day keeps the doctor away." And isn't that a good thing?

In both cases, it's just a habit. It's the same mechanism; assessing good and bad is up to us. When we remove judgment, we give ourselves a little bit of grace and understand how much of what we do is simply a result of how we're wired. It's just the way we are built. Habits are created out of necessity. Every life form does what is necessary.

There's nothing wrong with you. Read that again: There's nothing wrong with you! You are divine and perfect just the way you are! We need to tweak only a few things to allow ourselves to live in the vision of who we want to be and not a habitual reflection of our past.

❝ We need to tweak only a few things to allow ourselves to live in the vision of who we want to be, not a habitual reflection of our past.

How to break a destructive habit

Under the model of habit, the cue leads to the craving, which leads to the response, which leads to the reward. One of the easiest ways to change a habit is to hide the cue and make it hard to see, hear, smell, or touch. For instance, if you don't buy a bag of cookies from the grocery store and if they are not in your face in your kitchen, it makes it much harder to want cookies; you don't see them, so you don't eat them because you hid the cue.

Another thing you can do is make the response difficult. There was a time in medical school when I developed a daily habit of stopping at Whole Foods to get dinner on the way home. I would take the exit overpass, make the right turn, go into the parking lot, enter the store, walk around, and find something from the salad bar or other things throughout the store that I could take home to eat. I wasn't thinking ahead to shop for the week. I was thinking only of what I could scavenge for dinner. Most days, it wasn't a problem. I would go in and make myself a nice salad or whatever else. But on a stressful day, I might reach for the vegan ice cream or another suboptimal item. That was not helping me handle the underlying stress, and it was not a suitable coping mechanism. That daily Whole Foods addiction was something I had to address.

We tend to make decisions emotionally and justify them rationally; my justification was that it was Whole Foods! They have healthier alternatives and a salad bar!

However, what woke me up was when I was on my way home from medical school one day, driving down the highway. The next moment I was present and aware, I found myself at the checkout at Whole Foods! I didn't even recall taking the exit! I had turned into the Whole Foods parking lot, parked the car, got out, walked into the store, picked up a basket, went to the salad bar, filled it up with salad, grabbed some treats, and walked to the checkout line, all on complete autopilot. I looked down, and there was some good food, but others were not helpful. It was a shocking moment, to say the least!

That's when I realized I had to break the pattern because I did all of that unconsciously. It was all habit! I was zoned out, thinking about assignments, exams, or whatever was happening. I didn't even decide to take all the actions: the exit, right turn, parking lot, entering, walking around, making my selections. Of course, there's nothing wrong with Whole Foods. It's one of the best grocery stores, but you can get foods there that do not support your well-being if eaten in excess, and that's what I was doing.

I took an alternate route home for the next few weeks to break the habit cycle. By taking another way home, I was consciously telling myself it was okay to go to Whole Foods, but I would have to take the long way. This way, I wasn't restricting myself, thereby making me crave the rebellious action to get some unhealthy food anyway. And the long way was not often worth it due to the increased effort and time required. By making the response more difficult, it helped me break my habit.

What is it costing you to maintain a habit?
Are you struggling, or is someone around you struggling? Make it real in your mind. What is going to happen if you continue this way? What will be the outcome? Ultimately, the most important thing in changing a habit is to see yourself as somebody who lives above that standard. Make a conscious decision to hide what triggers the habit that isn't serving you or make it difficult to respond. Create a high standard and live above that so it becomes a piece of your identity. We'll discuss that more in chapter six.

This new view and standard is not "I have stopped smoking." It's: "I'm a nonsmoker." In another case, it might be, "I am responsible with my food," or "I am a healthy person." It's much harder to do unhealthy things when you see yourself as healthy; when you do that, the habit can no longer return.

Know what to do to form a constructive habit.

With any habit, we now know that the things that build a habit are the things that trigger the habit, so when you're talking about forming a constructive habit, one of the best resources I recommend to my clients is the book Atomic Habits by James Clear (2018), along with the Power of Habit by Charles Duhigg (2014). You can find these (and all the resources referenced in this book) on my website on a page created just for readers at drkarthikramanan.com/reader-resources. You  can also find them listed with the other sources and research in the appendix at the end of this publication.

These are excellent resources, so instead of rehashing their work, I will simply say that you can build slowly in small pieces when seeking to form a habit. That's the framework.

It is also essential to understand why it is crucial. Say you want to build a habit of walking every day. You plan to walk every morning, so you make your cue easy to see. You put your shorts, shirt, maybe even your jacket, and shoes by the bathroom so that when you wake up in the morning, you've got everything right there to get out the door and go for your walk. Making the cue visible makes the response convenient, which makes it easier to build a constructive habit.

But the other part is why you want to walk. It's not only because it's good to exercise or to get morning sunlight exposure to reset your circadian rhythm and maintain a robust body clock and hormone balance. It's also good to move your body because motion dictates emotion, my fifth pillar of emotional health.

Let's go deeper. Why? Why this? Ponder this perspective: walking ties into the person I want to be. The ideal version of myself is somebody who is more active. It's somebody who soaks in the sun every morning, and it's the person who walks despite the rain. It shows me that I act despite resistance. Every action is a vote toward the person I aspire to be, so when I want to build a habit, I want it to be a habit that is consistent with the person I want to be. We have to add emotion to it!

Reinforce your new habit of walking by playing some music on your headphones that inspires you, moves you, and energizes you in the way the ideal version of you would like. You want to tie positive emotion and power to all these habits you want to form. Do you want to eat better? All right, great. Why? Because you want to lose weight? Okay, that's good. Having a healthy body weight is good. But why? Why is it important to you?

When I talked to one of my clients about this, the initial answer was, "Well, I want to look good," Well, of course. But why? As we dug deeper into her purpose, we realized that she built her entire life around her physical ability to do what she wanted when she wanted to. Her father made her do a lot of hard work growing up. She moved a lot, tearing things down and cleaning up, so she learned to navigate those situations when things became challenging. Now, later in life, she realized that one of her passions is helping people make certain difficult parts of their lives easier.

Okay, what does this have to do with building constructive habits and eating better? As we continued talking, once she realized what her deepest passion and purpose were tied to, she realized she wanted to have that impact for many years. She wanted to watch her kids grow and become a grandparent while positively impacting her community. She wanted to be healthy and happy deep into her life. She wanted to live to 90 and beyond to live her purpose longer. She wanted her life to mean more for as long as possible.

Living with a purposeful vision makes it much easier to say, "I will eat better." You want to form constructive habits around your food. (Pillar Number Three of Emotional Health: Nutrition.) So all of a sudden, it's not, "Oh, I can't have the brownie. I have to eat the salad." Instead, it's exciting! "I eat a lot of whole plants because I want to live a long and healthy life. Then I can continue to make a difference for others around me."

You form a constructive habit with a visible cue, an attractive craving, an easy response, and an enticing reward. Beyond that, there has to be a strong why. When you decide to live into your purpose and want health for longevity – not just lifespan, but healthspan – you tie powerful emotion to your efforts, and building a constructive habit becomes much easier to execute.

What is the framework for maximizing habits?
The framework for maximizing your habits is to set up your environment so that you can live into your vision of the person you want to be.

Your environment is your physical space. It's your timespace. It's your social space. It's your mental space. It's your nutritional space. It's your schedule, your calendar. All of these factors in your environment drastically affect your behavior.

Willpower is difficult to acquire. We can force ourselves to do a certain amount for a while, but eventually, it has to be natural. That's what we're talking about here with maximizing frameworks. Maximizing habits means maximizing the environmental potential of allowing us to use that cue, craving, response, and reward in the constructive manner we desire.

Removing obstacles is one of the best ways to maximize any habit you want to build. Imagine you have a piece of furniture that is always in the way. Then, one day, you break your toe on it. No matter what treatments you receive, if you keep stubbing your toe on that piece of furniture regularly, your toe won't heal. You must remove the obstacle and create space to walk around that piece of furniture. If you always have cookies in your pantry or sitting out on the counter, the willpower needed to refrain from eating that cookie is significant. However, when the cookie is not in the house, not eating a cookie becomes much more manageable.

You want to set up your environment to facilitate your becoming the person you want to be so that habits become easier to break, make, and maintain. To maximize your habits, ensure the positive cues are right in front of you, and the negative cues are as hidden as possible. Similarly, when you want to break one, you should set up your environment so those cues are not in front of you.

Look at the various aspects of your life—your physical space, the people with whom you spend the most time, the food options around you, your bedroom environment, your digital environment (including your social media)—and facilitate your environment to support becoming your ideal self.

CHAPTER 6

Expectations versus Standards

The Framework for Joy

Let's say you're trying to win over a client, or it's your anniversary or another occasion where you want to give the other person an incredibly memorable experience. Think about your favorite go-to restaurant for such occasions. When you make this reservation for this dinner, how would you characterize your expectations? Most likely, your expectations are high because you're going to a nice, expensive restaurant and are confident it will be a tremendous experience.

You're pleased to find your server is on the ball. He offers food recommendations and drink suggestions. You never had to wait for anything, but at the same time, he isn't helicoptering either. He fills your water before you even realize it is running low and always asks you a question at just the right time without interrupting your conversation. You have a flawless experience. Your dinner guests love it; you make an incredible impression and a fantastic, long-lasting memory!

Your expectations were high, and your reality played out above those expectations, as lofty as they were. So how do you feel? You likely feel happy, excited, and maybe even relieved! You feel positive emotions all around.

Now, let's say your server is having a bad night when you arrive with your guest. He's late getting your order, looks flustered, and seems to be juggling too much. Maybe he even spills a drink on your guest. Your order is wrong, and you must wait for your tab long after your meal ends.

In this scenario, the situation has fallen below your expectations, so how do you feel? You likely feel upset, angry, sad, and disappointed. You experience negative emotions.

What's the problem here?
The problem is that we've allowed factors outside our control to dictate our emotional state. When our expectations are high, this is the nature of expectations. The range of outcomes that enable us to be happy is minimal.

Meanwhile, the range of outcomes that upset us, making us angry, sad, or miserable, is more extensive.

When I talk to high-achieving individuals, whether business owners or corporate professionals, they often have high expectations of themselves and their team. Then, when things don't unfold as expected, they get frustrated with themselves and those around them, and they may experience unpleasant emotions at home and work.

Let's do some second-order thinking here. What happens when a leader shows up to those around them with frustration, disappointment, stress, or other nonconstructive emotions? How do the people around this individual react? If we consistently show up to our teams and families this way, how long will they want to stay around us? How much inspired action can we create? Setting high expectations breeds disappointment.

The key is to lower expectations, which might be a hard pill for many of us. My former self was one such person! I suggest you lower your expectations of your employees, clients, vendors, and family, and most importantly, lower your expectations of yourself. Many of us are perfectionists. We want to do things with excellence. But the truth is that even when we do something flawlessly as a perfectionist, it still isn't good enough because we have set the bar for ourselves so impossibly high that even when we meet it, it doesn't matter. We're on to the next thing. We don't take a moment to sincerely acknowledge and celebrate the journey, the moments, and the people who helped, supported, or achieved with us.

Where is the joy in that? High expectations lead to more stress and frustration, and everybody loses. Lower your expectations!

I can hear you already! "Dr. K, I don't want to be mediocre! We're in it to win!" Of course you are! I am, too. We don't want our clients to have a subpar experience, and we don't want our families to be anything less than happy, but we can have that without raising our expectations to unattainable levels.

This is where standards come into play. Expectations drive how you feel in response to a situation. Usually, these situations are outside of your control. On the other hand, standards dictate what you will and will not tolerate going forward.

Let's go back to the example at the restaurant. You've been to this restaurant dozens of times. You've taken a lot of people here, and it has always been phenomenal. This one time, it went poorly, so maybe you give it another shot for the next special dinner. Let's say it goes well the next time, so you chalk up the previous negative experience as a weird anomaly.

But what if it goes poorly again? After all those positive experiences, now you have two negative ones in a row. What are you going to do? You're probably not going back ever again.

That's what raising standards looks like. Standards are what we will and will not tolerate going forward and are within your control.

❝ Expectations drive how you feel in response to a situation and are usually beyond your control. Standards dictate what you will and will not tolerate going forward and are within your control.

Lower Your Expectations and Raise Your Standards

Imagine an instance where you have an employee who, despite what you felt was good training, just made a mistake. With the typical high-expectation way of doing things, this individual fell below your expectations, so you're frustrated and may have expressed as much to this person. That might motivate some people to learn and grow. But for others, it may lead them into a sympathetic nervous system state – fight, flight, freeze – and maybe shrink away, lose respect for you, or seek a new job.

Instead, you can pause and look at the situation rationally when you lower your expectations. You're able to think this through. "If I blow up on this person, what is the likelihood they will learn from this?" We can then diagnose the actual issue. Was the training inadequate? Did this individual have the opportunity to ask enough questions? Are they having a bad day, and this mistake was an aberration? Or did we hire the right person but for the wrong role?

When we're stressed by high expectations, we can't rationally consider any of this. However, with lowered expectations, we can make the best next choice. We can ask the right questions, letting the individual know that we're invested in their learning and growth and that we believe in them. The long-term result? Often, the employee learns and grows, whether in the current role or another one.

What happens if the individual continues to fall below the standard set for the role? At that point, we can determine whether their skillset is better suited to a different position or whether they would be more successful working for a different company. Both parties can move forward with a more favorable outcome.

How does this framework relate to our patterns within ourselves? Let's say you're a working professional, and you are hungry to move up the ranks and advance your career. You're a perfectionist in everything you do; nothing ever feels good enough. Lowering our expectations of ourselves allows us to make mistakes. After all, we learn more from our mistakes than our victories. Instead of beating ourselves up, we take the opportunity to grow.

High standards relate to what we will tolerate of ourselves. Instead of expecting an outcome that might be outside our control (for example, we can put ourselves in a position for a promotion, but the choice is not up to us), we craft a vision of how we approach the process, how we want to handle people and projects, and how we want to treat our bodies and minds. We create an environment internally and externally that allows us to live in the vision of our ideal selves.

In time, those high standards translate into greater outward success; we allow ourselves the grace necessary to focus on other important areas of life, especially our health and relationships.

Too many of us walk through life without a clear sense of purpose, which wears on us over time. The problem is not the nine-to-five; it's the standards in our lives that result in a lack of purpose and growth, which could stand to be raised.

When we raise the standard for ourselves, we allow others to set high standards for themselves. What do they stand for? What do they want to be known for? What do they want to be remembered for? What do they want their life to mean?

Lower your expectations. Raise your standards. That's the framework for joy.

❚❚ Lower your expectations. Raise your standards. That's the framework for joy.

Why do we tolerate suboptimal people, environments, and truths in our lives?

Change is hard and takes energy. Think about that friend who is continually toxic. You might reach the point where you think, "I love this person, but I need to put some space between us right now." Think about how difficult that conversation can be. Where do we even start? How do we bring this subject up at all? It takes energy.

What about that job a person hates? They feel trapped because they have a certain standard of living that would take a hit if they left that job. Facing uncertainty takes energy. We aren't wired to want to spend energy unnecessarily, and that's why we tolerate a suboptimal life. The pain we're experiencing may be less than the perceived pain of making the change. And eventually, like all living things, we change when it hurts enough.

Notice I said "perceived pain," not "actual pain." How often have we stressed out over an upcoming exam, a date, a work project, or a business meeting just to realize afterward that it wasn't as bad as we thought it would be?

Raising our standards, while it still requires effort, is not as scary or daunting as we think it will be. Want to get healthy? Instead of "I have to lose 30 pounds", focus on "What do I need to do to be the healthiest version of me today?"

Instead of feeling defeated with your business and focusing on how hard it'll be to shift your business plan to produce more revenue and profits, break down the steps necessary to get to your desired result, figure out how many leads you'll need and how many sales you'll need to make to get to that result, and then execute one step at a time. Remember, you can control the action, not the result, because results are outside our control, but we can control our actions.

Instead of thinking about how long and hard it'll be to write that book, focus on the message you're trying to convey, reverse engineer the journey while outlining the chapters, and then plug away one chapter at a time. (Yes, I also needed to remind myself of this approach when writing this very book!)

When it comes to our health and especially our relationships, it can be daunting to think about all the things we "should" do. Eat better. Exercise more. Go to therapy. Get some sleep. Spend time with loved ones. Oh yeah, but don't slack in your work, either.

Raising our standards means focusing on one thing at a time. What if improving our sleep gives us more energy to exercise? What if exercising makes us not want to reach for that junk food? What if eating better makes us feel better about ourselves? What if feeling better about ourselves leads to more fulfilling interactions with others?

See how this works? Yes, we change when it hurts enough, but why wait until then? How long will that take? Five years? Ten years? Twenty?

Something we don't measure when weighing the pain of the current situation versus the perceived pain of changing is the cost of keeping things the same. What will happen to your health? Your relationships? What is it costing you not to raise your standards in life? What will it cost your loved ones for you not to raise your standards? What will it cost you to keep living the way you are?

Too often, we stay in a holding pattern, hoping things will improve. We hope this business turns around, this marriage gets better, or our job becomes more fulfilling. Hope is important because without it, we cannot believe in a better future and cannot take action toward that better future. I'm sorry to say, however, that hope alone is not a strategy! We need to link that hope with a plan. We need to marry that hope with raised standards.

We can also change by crafting a vision of the person we want to be, one with elevated standards, and then taking one step toward becoming that person today. It truly is that simple.

How to Set Strong Standards

To set strong standards, start with the end in mind. What do we want out of life? What do we want our life to mean? Go deeper. What do you really want?

Years ago, I said I wanted to be healthy and have a good-looking body. I wanted to lose weight, but what did I really want? It wasn't about the weight. It was about self-image. Why did I want a positive self-image? I wanted to feel confident. Why did I want to feel confident? So that I could find the right woman with whom to share my life. And why did I want the right woman in my life? Because I wanted companionship and love more than anything else. And why did I want companionship and love from her? Because I didn't feel love towards myself.

That was the actual root desire. I wanted to feel unconditional love towards myself. Eventually, I did lose 100 pounds, which was my original desire: to be healthy and have a good-looking body. But the self-criticism was still alive and well. At the time, I hadn't dug deeper into the root craving: unconditional self-love.

I wanted unconditional self-love. Once I reached that place, I met the love of my life. We started our lives together while supporting each other through building our businesses to fulfill our purposes in this world. Then, it became even more apparent that there was another level to explore. I wanted my life to be about helping others find their own emotional health, inner peace, and life purpose. And that sets the standard for everything I do.

Ask yourself what you want. Keep asking yourself why this

matters to you. As you dig deeper, you may realize there are further layers to purpose. Once you get to the root, let that be the starting point for your new standards. What do you need to stop tolerating from yourself and your environment? What do you need to stop tolerating in order to grow?

Every thought we think, every action we take, every piece of food we put in our mouth, every time we commit to sleeping rather than staying up too late, every person we choose to spend time with or not spend time with, every choice we make or don't make are all a vote towards the person we want to be. Therein lie our standards.

If that strategy seems challenging to implement, consider what I call the Regret Formula.

The Regret Formula

Imagine you wake up one morning at 92 years old and reflect on your life. What would you regret? Would you regret not starting that business? Would you regret not asking that person out? Would you regret not focusing on your health or investing your money earlier? What are all the things you would regret if you didn't do? Write those down, or use the worksheet I've created for you, available on the reader resources page of my website:  drk-arthikramanan.com/reader-resources.

Now, envision a "no-regret" version of yourself—someone who pursued their dreams, expressed how they felt to the people they loved the most, and made a difference in the lives of others.

Whether you ask "Why?" over and over until you reach your root craving and purpose or use the Regret Formula, craft a vision right now of your ideal self and establish the standards by which this ideal version of you lives!

CHAPTER SEVEN

Boundaries Made Better

What you tolerate continues

As harsh as it may sound, we get what we tolerate in life.

In chapter six, we explored raising standards and lowering expectations. When we want to understand our current boundaries, we need to observe what we tolerate (and perhaps no longer will). It may not have to do with other people; it could be something as mundane as the daily tasks we do repeatedly that make our lives a little harder.

For instance, if we don't have an organizational system in our kitchen and have very little healthy food at home, putting a meal together that serves our well-being becomes difficult. That added resistance of rummaging to find the right knife and discovering you don't have the ingredient you want for the recipe makes us feel a little bit more stressed each time we look for something to make and eat. As a result, we'll lean towards something quicker to grab. Instead of spending five minutes assembling a colorful and gigantic salad, we reach for the crackers, and the poor nutrition outcome is what we get because we tolerate it.

What about that friend group member who often kills the conversation with a topic nobody wants to engage in? At first, we and our other friends give each other the eye, hoping this awkward moment will pass. And maybe it does. But then it happens the next time. And the time after that. Eventually, everyone is dealing with this individual's topic without having a compassionate conversation with them about why it might be a good idea to tone down said topic. Unfortunately, we tolerate it and continue the exposure.

So what's the solution? Boundaries, of course! Perhaps you've seen this topic discussed regarding family members, friends, or coworkers.

I'm going to say something controversial here. I'm not a fan of boundaries, the way they are typically portrayed.

Here's an example: Let's say Albert has an issue with his sister Kate. They miscommunicated about their elderly parents, triggering personal truths from years past. Kate feels Albert always dismisses her, and Albert feels Kate always gets her way with their parents. Perhaps Albert and Kate went to social media independently to seek advice and were told they needed better boundaries. So what do they do? They don't talk to each other anymore.

Ten years go by, and their mother passes away. Albert and Kate meet awkwardly at the funeral. Their spouses and children can feel the tension, as it's uncomfortable for them too. They want to catch up with people but feel pulled into a family dynamic they didn't even create.

In this example, firm boundaries solved the short-term issue of Albert and Kate's emotionally charged arguments, but did they do more harm than good in the long run?

When we have limited parts of the information puzzle, we complete it by filling in the missing pieces instinctively based on the truths we possess about ourselves and the world around us. We "bridge the information gap" in alignment with the lens through which we see the world. Remember the earlier example of coming home to the tipped-over fish bowl and happy cat? Just like we completed that story, we do this all the time, usually without knowing we're doing it.

When we apply the concept of bridging the information gap,

are we doing so with the most likely outcome or more extreme aftereffects? When my dog Toby manages to escape the house to take himself on a walk through the neighborhood, even though he's never gone far and my wife and I have found him 100% of the times before, a horrible feeling courses through my body each time. "What if I never see him again? What if I find him run over by a car? Or attacked by a coyote?" Is that the most likely outcome? No. But when we don't have all the data, our minds are wired to assume the worst because, out in nature, assuming the worst allows us to survive. "Oh, that rustling in the leaves is probably just a squirrel. It can't possibly be a tiger." No, we'll assume it's a tiger until proven otherwise. And that's good for survival! It's just not great for personal relationships.

If Albert and Kate don't talk for ten years, will they think about each other in the most favorable light? Unlikely. And what's the payoff? The destructive truths that they hold about each other remain true. They can say, "I told you so." But is that the best outcome? Does it serve their well-being, their relationship, or their family dynamic?

A better way to look at boundaries

When you think of the word "boundary," do you think of a flexible yet mostly firm set of rules that facilitates the best results while keeping out only the undesired results? Or do you think of "The Wall" from Game of Thrones, a 700-foot-tall, 300-foot-thick, 300-mile-long impenetrable barrier, cold as ice? I don't know about you, but it sounds more like the latter to me. Does that create the results we want?

Instead, what if we expanded our boundaries to become the line we will not cross no matter what? These self-declared rules would be in line with our morals and values. Under no circumstances will we, for instance, rob a bank. They can also apply to more trivial things. For example, we'll never walk into an important business meeting without brushing our teeth that morning.

Boundaries can be the outermost guideposts to who we are and who we are not. They're crucial for creating a strong sense of identity.

It's important to know that this has nothing to do with what's "right" or "wrong." These are subjective terms. If someone dealt with alcohol addiction in the past and has found a better life by completely abstaining from alcohol, that's their boundary. However, If their friend enjoys a mixed drink occasionally, their boundary doesn't exclude the infrequent drink. That's ok. We each are living our own journey and can craft our individual boundaries.

To inventory your current boundaries, think about those absolutes in your life. What will you uphold no matter what? What will you not engage in, regardless of the circumstances? What do you stand for at all costs, and why? Notice what you feel as a firm "yes" or "no" over the next week or two. Consider the broadest barriers you will or will not cross under almost any circumstance. These are your firm boundaries, aligning with the person you want to be and the life you want to create.

The More Flexible Approach for a Better Life

As we move inward from the rigid boundaries, we still want to create space and structure to live into the vision of our ideal selves. This might include having that uncomfortable conversation with that one person in the friend group we discussed earlier. It might involve reaching out to a family member to express how you feel and what you hope the relationship can become. It might mean consciously giving yourself grace when life's happenings fall below your expectations.

Instead of rigid boundaries, as others typically describe them, the concept of standards discussed in the previous chapter allow us to move toward a more fulfilling, emotionally healthy life while preserving the flexibility to make one-off decisions.

As people-pleasers (yes, I was one before), we too often say yes to anyone and everything. We want to make life better for those around us, but we may not see that we tolerate people who take advantage of our kindness. Again, we get more of what we tolerate.

What if, instead, the standard was that we take care of ourselves so that we are the best we can be to take care of others? When we get on the plane, what do the flight attendants tell us about the oxygen masks? Put yours on before you put one on someone who needs your help. The worst-case scenario unfolds if we run out of oxygen while fiddling with another person's mask. Instead, when we quickly and efficiently take care of ourselves, we're in better shape to take care of others.

Does that mean we always say no by putting ourselves first, no matter the situation? If "I get to come first now" is a boundary, the answer is yes. We might ignore a legitimate need of a family member, a friend silently crying out for help, or a coworker who needs a hand and would genuinely appreciate and remember your efforts. But if our standard is that we are here to serve others when not at the expense of ourselves, then we get to figure out each situation on a case-by-case basis.

I have built a business around helping business owners, their companies, and growth-seeking individuals achieve unshakeable emotional health so they can find and live into their life purpose. I pour more emotional energy into others than I would have imagined possible earlier in life, and I love every minute of it!

Yet, there are moments when I listen to my body and recognize that I need to slow down, disconnect, and give my brain a break. For me, this might include playing relatively mindless games, watching entertaining YouTube videos, or living by my favorite movie line from the scene in Office Space where Michael asks Peter what he did the whole weekend. Peter says, "I did nothing. I did absolutely nothing, and it was everything that I thought it could be."

Unfortunately, when I have these blocks of time to disconnect and do nothing, I sometimes miss last-minute invitations with people I care deeply about. I have explained to them the nature of what I do and that my decompression time is a part of my productivity because, without it, I'm less than helpful to my clients. They get it. My preferred course of action is to schedule quality time with them in advance so that I can schedule decompression time around those events that matter most.

However, occasionally, something important comes up, and my wife, another family member, or a friend needs something more urgently that I can help with. At that moment, they become the priority. If my self-care were a rigid boundary, I would say no and lose a chance to make a difference for someone I care about. But because it's a standard, I can be flexible and assess each situation for what it is.

Allow your standards to dictate what you will and will not tolerate going forward. Drive your standards by your vision of the ideal self and the life you desire. Use those standards as a blueprint to navigate life's choices. It's not about rigidity or right and wrong. It's about zooming out so our micro actions align with our macro vision for our lives.

❚❚ Zoom out so your micro-actions align with your macro vision for your life.

How to set healthy standards and boundaries without damaging relationships

It's easy to want to set rigid boundaries and cut people out of our lives. It's a little more difficult to pull that off. It's even more challenging to deal with some long-term secondary effects of establishing a rigid boundary rather than a flexible standard. That's especially true with relationships.

Let's take the story of Jane. Jane had a lifelong history of dealing with her mother's criticism. No matter what Jane did or how much she achieved, her mother always seemed to have something snide to say. It affected her well into adulthood. At a certain point, all Jane wanted to do was cut off her mother from her life. And for a short time, she chose to try it. What happened? More criticism and more guilt-tripping. Her mother would leave passive-aggressive text messages about how she missed Jane, followed by something sharp and critical, often in the same sentence. It's easy to want to step away from this person.

But what was the relationship Jane desired to have with her mother? Jane said she just wanted to have a kind and compassionate relationship. It didn't have to be fancy. She no longer needed her mother's approval, as she had done the work to own her past and start living in the vision of her ideal, strong, vibrant self. She just wanted to enjoy the years she had left with her mother, no matter how that would look.

We can't guarantee the outcome when we raise our standards around those we love. We can't change anyone else; we can only control our intentions and actions. But we can influence others by how we show up to those relationships.

Remember the lens through which we see the world? Jane's mother had her own view. As Jane and I talked through her mother's life experiences, it became clear that her mother experienced challenges with Jane's grandmother. When Jane put herself in her mother's shoes, she realized she might have ended up the same way as her mother did and that Jane may have followed in the footsteps of her lineage if she didn't choose to work on herself instead. With that compassion, Jane began checking in on her mother, asking how her mom was feeling and what was happening in her world. She made a point to spend time together in small bursts to maintain her well-being in the moment. Over time, Jane's mother opened up more, lowering her walls and becoming more vulnerable. Will she ever get to the point of high self-awareness and inner healing? It's up to Jane's mother to do that work. But Jane came to a place where she was at peace with her relationship with her mother, and they were able to have some of that quality time that Jane wanted from the start.

When raising our standards with others, we must consider how they see the world. What might the other person have experienced or be experiencing that affects their emotional health? How can we elevate ourselves so we might positively influence them? What if we reimagined our interactions with these people closest to us, crafting a better way of being that allows us to become our ideal selves while holding the candle for those around us to illuminate who they can become? They may begin to see you in a different light than how they perceived you in the past and treat you how you want to be treated.

Notice I said they may see you in a different light. It also may not happen as sometimes, when we grow, people around us feel we're leaving them behind. When I was on my weight loss journey through healthy eating, I had a small handful of friends who said I was getting too skinny. Mind you, I was still 40 pounds overweight at the time. In no world was I too skinny. Thankfully, these were friends I felt comfortable slowly distancing myself from. They wanted different things in life than where I was going, and that's okay. We're all on our own journey.

If they had been family members, I wouldn't have wanted to cut them out of my life. I would have told myself that this is just who they are right now. I can still show up as the best version of myself, sharing my excitement and vision for life with them and allowing those interactions to have their own results.

Each person and relationship is different. There's no one formula for raising your standards without damaging relationships. But as long as we live in the vision of our ideal selves and shine our light brightly, maybe, just maybe, we'll inspire those around us to take their first steps to become a growth seeker.

CHAPTER EIGHT

Perfectionism, Imposter Syndrome, and Self-Criticism

How you measure up depends on what you measure

We've now discussed the lens through which we see the world and understand why we think and act the way we do. We've learned the framework for joy, explored standards vs. expectations, and learned a new way of establishing boundaries.

Let me ask you this: Have you ever listened to a podcast, read a book, or attended a seminar where you learned many incredible tools and gained tons of inspiration, only to find yourself right back where you started two weeks later?

I love motivation, and I love inspiration! Unfortunately, a motivational speech, a podcast, or a book (even this one) doesn't shift those truths that run our lives. However, those sources of knowledge allow us to open ourselves to new possibilities, ways of doing things, and ways of being that we may not have believed possible before. And once that curiosity strikes, especially if it coincides with the pain produced by life's circumstances, we change.

❝ Unfortunately, those truths that run our lives aren't shifted by a motivational speech, a podcast, or a book.

Think about an ice cube at zero degrees Fahrenheit. Put it in the sun, apply heat, and watch it melt. In this case, you are warming it with self-help resources: podcasts, seminars, and books. Five degrees, ten degrees. Perhaps you start going to therapy and make tremendous progress in understanding your past and navigating your current feelings. Fifteen degrees, twenty degrees. But you still seem right where you were, just like the ice cube is still an ice cube, but now at 20 degrees. So you think the next book or seminar will get you there. Twenty-three, twenty-five degrees. The ice cube is still an ice cube, so was all this work for nothing? Not at all. The latent potential energy of the ice cube is changing, even if you can't see it.

You sense something is still missing, even as you feel you've progressed. You may notice that you lean further into your perfectionistic tendencies when stress arises. After all, that's what got you to this success in life.

As the pressure mounts, maybe imposter syndrome rears its ugly head, making you feel uneasy, questioning whether you're good enough to take on this new challenge at work or pursue a new opportunity. Perhaps as things get more painful, that negative voice in your head harasses you incessantly, becoming louder and more vicious. Being hard on ourselves might be how we've achieved success in life. It might also have led to unhealthy coping mechanisms like addiction.

Human beings, like all living things, change when it hurts enough. Often, the challenges we face can drive incredible change if we respond with emotional resilience.

Imagine a basketball dropped from hip height. How high will it bounce back? At best, it'll bounce back to the level it fell from. Now imagine spiking the basketball, raising it above your head, and throwing it down with all your might. You still release it from hip level, but how high does it bounce now? It's much higher than a regular bounce!

When we become emotionally resilient, like the basketball in this example, the challenges we face in life shape us into who we can be. Despite our biological urge to avoid it, pain is our greatest teacher.

❝ Pain is our greatest teacher

In those painful moments, we can seize the opportunity to take the next step in our journey. The ice cube has seven degrees to go before it becomes water, and in our journey, those last seven degrees may take a different type of work at the right time with the right method and the right people. But as it happens, we transform. We become water. We become free.

Perfectionism

On the surface, perfectionism seems like an excellent trait to possess. After all, with a perfectionist mindset, we do great work and often reap great rewards. However, as we might in any situation, we must ask ourselves, "What is perfectionism costing me?" My perfectionism led to success in my corporate career. It led to a refinement of skills in anything to which I fully committed. But it also led to applying less than total effort into anything I felt I couldn't perfect. Worst of all, even when I reached lofty goals, it never felt good enough. Perfectionism removed my ability to enjoy the fruits of my efforts. It dissolved the focus that would have enhanced the process and allowed me to enjoy the journey.

At its core, perfectionism is an extremely high expectation of ourselves. We desire a perfect result. Actions are within our control, but results are merely influenced and never chosen. When factors outside our control affect an outcome, we set ourselves up for disappointment.

Why does that perfectionistic mentality exist in the first place? First, look into your truths. Which truths about yourself do perfectionism reinforce? Which stories about the reality in which you live play into your need to be perfect? What does it mean about you if you are not perfect? Stop reading and think about your answer to that question, and when you answer it, ask yourself, "Why?" again. Dig deep into that idea. And perhaps again, ask why to go one level deeper.

We must remember that most thoughts, patterns, behaviors, and actions are rooted in our unconscious mind. Just because we have always been a certain way does not mean we have to remain that way, and it certainly does not mean that continuing this way will lead to the inner peace and joy we seek in life.

Raise your standards rather than succumbing to the compulsive need to be perfect because of what you think it means about you or others' perception of you. Raise your standards around effort and mentality. Raise your standards for asking yourself the right questions to refine your approach. Raise your standards for achieving the same performance outcome without negatively impacting your emotional health.

Imposter Syndrome

In my third year of medical school, after two grueling years and passing our first board exams, my classmates and I were finally able to see patients in the medical school's teaching clinic. We were assigned to be either "secondary" or "primary" students based on our experience level, and we worked under the license of the attending physician. We eagerly awaited this moment after the countless hours of studying, the difficult exams, and the emotional strain of losing friends who failed out of the program along the way. We finally got to sit in a room with a patient and had the opportunity to help a real person!

Despite having gone through my life-changing weight loss experience and journey to emotional health, I could not shake the feeling that I had made it here by accident. I felt like a fraud. I looked around my class and saw many brilliant minds. In my "free time" after studying hard, I was busy being President of the Student Government Association, developing my speaking skills, and networking with doctors in the field. Many class-mates spent extra hours studying or in clubs, which enhanced their clinical skills. I felt like I didn't match up to them. There was so much I didn't know yet! (It turns out everyone had quite a bit they had yet to learn!) When it was time to come back to the clinic classroom and report back to the attending physi-cian on my list of differential diagnoses, my thought process on which further tests I would run, and what my possible treat-ment plans would be, I felt like an absolute imposter.

Imposter syndrome hit me hard, and I would not shake it for quite some time.

Psychologists Pauline Rose Clance and Suzanne Imes coined the term "Imposter Syndrome" in 1978 while studying 150 high-performing women who persistently felt like intellectual frauds despite their success and achievements. The women in the study believed their success was attributed to luck or fooling others about their capabilities. The researchers attributed this behavior to societal messages that women did not belong in posi-tions of power. Later research determined this phenomenon af-fected others independent of gender, settings, and other factors.

While imposter syndrome is not a diagnosable medical con-dition, it is a common psychological phenomenon. It is espe-cially common among high-achieving professionals and entre-preneurs, and often, the more successful people get, the more imposter syndrome can rear its head.

There are several signs of imposter syndrome. You might downplay your performance, overachieve, or self-sabotage. You might feel you're not as competent as others perceive you to be. You might experience crippling self-doubt. You might attribute your success to external factors, almost as if you succeeded by accident. It might be difficult for you to take a heartfelt compli-ment. And my favorite (because this was me) is you might set the bar unrealistically high so that you can fall short.

Imposter syndrome is a vicious cycle. You don't feel good enough, so you overachieve to produce outstanding results and avoid being "found out." You'll get success, accolades, and appreciation, which makes you feel like more of a fraud. That leads you to continue to overachieve. And on and on we go.

Much like perfectionism (which can coincide with imposter syndrome), it's important to understand what we're attempting to prove true by feeling like an imposter. What life experiences made us feel like we're not good enough? How did we learn to compensate for that sentiment through outworking and out-achieving others? How has this served us in some ways? How has it hindered us in other ways? And what if we stepped out of our subjective reality and saw ourselves the way those who love and admire us the most see us?

I'm sure you have a friend or family member who is extraordinary at what they do, and they're the last person to give themselves credit. No matter how much you praise and appreciate them, they can't take compliments or positive sentiments because it conflicts with their sense of self—their truth about themselves. Yet, you still believe in this person no matter what, correct?

The same applies to you. We can't have double standards. We can either believe we are imposters or see ourselves the way others who love and respect us the most see us. Their truth is that you are incredible. Who is to say their truth is any less valid than yours?

Reality is subjective. We get to decide how we see ourselves. You can choose the disempowering reality, or you can choose the empowering reality. The power is yours.

Later in my medical training, I primed myself to pay attention to signs that I was better than I thought. After all, I sought evidence to prove the "truth" that I was an imposter. Now, I

> **We get to decide how we see ourselves. You can choose the disempowering reality, or you can choose the empowering reality. The choice, and the power, is yours.**

would focus on the opposite signs I had previously dismissed. Sometimes, as doctors, our patients can lead to our healing, and on one random Thursday in March of my last year of medical school, that is what happened.

I walked up to the reception area to get my patient (we'll call him Greg), whom I had been treating with weekly therapies under the supervision of an attending physician for some months. That day, Greg and I walked down the hall to the treatment room and ran into my attending physician. Greg turned to her and said, "Doctor, do you mind if I forego my treatment today? I just want to talk to him." I stood flabbergasted as this gentle, struggling 57-year-old man pointed at me with the kindest look. "Sure, absolutely!" she said.

It was at that moment that my imposter syndrome melted away. We can compare our skills to the skills of others, and when we do, we typically measure ourselves against the best. When we feel like imposters, this is how we craft a narrative in our minds that we are, in fact, less than. That day, Greg showed me many facets of being a physician. Yes, diagnosis and treatment are vital, and the reality was that I was well above average in those areas, whether I wanted to admit it or not. But Greg showed me that my superpower was knowing how to be present with him, listen to him, and celebrate him, even when he didn't want to for himself. He helped me realize I allowed him to feel heard, seen, and loved for who he was. We had an incredible conversation that day, and I'll forever be grateful to him for believing in me and for his contribution to my life. Rest in peace, Greg. Thank you for believing in me.

Self-Criticism

Self-doubt is good. Remember, we were optimized for nature. Would self-doubt be helpful in nature? Yes, and here's why.

"What if I can't make it across that river?"

"I don't think I can outrun that giant cat with stripes."

See my point? Self-doubt is there to protect us from danger, and that can be useful. Imagine our modern world if we didn't have the self-protection mechanism of doubt as it relates to walking across a busy street with speeding cars or whether we can pass a test without studying.

Self-doubt may hit us harder than what might be rationally justified. We might doubt our ability to make a good video for social media if we're trying to make it as a business owner or creator. However, there's a difference between doubting ourselves and knowing we are worthless, not good enough, and undeserving of love from anyone, including ourselves.

If you've ever doubted yourself, that's not what I'm referring to when discussing self-criticism. I'll say this: Self-criticism is a lens through which we see the world that brightens everyone and everything else and darkens the mirrors in which we see our own reflections.

> **Self-criticism is a lens through which we see the world that brightens everyone and everything else and darkens the mirrors in which we see our own reflections.**

It can show up as that negative voice in our heads constantly demeaning us, telling us we're not good enough, and calling us an idiot. There isn't a moment that goes by when we're intensely self-critical, where we give ourselves credit or appreciate ourselves for who we are and how far we've come.

It may concurrently affect us with anxiety, depression, and, yes, perfectionism and imposter syndrome. It may rob us of meaningful relationships, as we're always giving the other person credit for everything that goes right and making ourselves wrong for everything that goes wrong.

None of us were born self-critical. Have you ever watched a baby learn how to walk? Do they walk perfectly the first time they try? They stumble, fall, get up, stumble, and fall again. If they had the self-critical mentality that we can develop as adults, they'd say, "Well, I guess walking isn't for me!"

As kids, we're inherently filled with wonder. Then, due to life's happenings, traumas, and others' truths imparted onto us, we begin to place guardrails on ourselves. That's essentially true for most people. Those who are self-critical take it a step further. We make someone else's critical voice our own. Perhaps someone said we'll never amount to anything, or we're incapable or not good enough, and at some point, that becomes our inner voice. That voice isn't the truth. We learned it. And, much like other self-protecting mechanisms meant for nature, it's there to protect us.

Someone painted a picture of a world where we aren't enough, imparting a "truth," so we build various forms of armor to protect ourselves from this "reality," including that negative voice in our heads that tells us not to try that sport, apply for that job, or ask that person out. The same negative voice makes us feel unworthy of love, so we don't risk telling others, "I love you." The voice rejects us before we can even put ourselves out there to experience the fear of rejection.

We might fight with that voice. We might condemn it. We might hate it. But when we get a paper cut, do we blame our skin for failing us? Do we fight it, get mad at it? Or do we wash it, apply an antibiotic as needed, and bandage it? Why do we treat a physical wound differently than an emotional wound?

That voice is here to protect us. When I was dealing with my self-critical voice, in addition to EMDR (eye-movement desensitization and reprocessing) therapy, I made a point to notice that voice and say, "Thank you. I know you're just trying to protect me. I'm okay, and I'm doing this."

We may think of traumas as significant painful experiences that scar us, and yet traumas can seem innocuous by whatever social standards we live. Trauma is simply an emotional response to an event that overwhelms our current coping mechanisms and is an area where a therapy like EMDR can be powerful in reprocessing those events with current-day coping skills and perspectives.

If you have experienced trauma, I highly recommend seeking out a local counselor trained in trauma thera-  py. For professionals certified in EMDR, visit em-dria.org/find-an-emdr-therapist/ or look for the link on the reader resources page of my website.

As we go through our healing journey, look at life's events and the outcomes they created. And I mean the good along with the bad. We most certainly focus on the adverse effects of our experiences in life, and for good reason: we must protect ourselves from those situations happening again, and that's vital. At the same time, we may apply what we have learned in areas that may not warrant it, inhibiting us from our true potential. And if we're honest with ourselves, where did our superpowers come from? Ponder that one for yourself. Would your superpowers be as strong if your life unfolded differently?

We can't change the past. But we can change how we look at the past, the lessons we've learned, and the meaning we take from it. Therein lies our ability to shift our inner truth from disempowering to empowering.

I know it can be scary to face ourselves. I won't pretend it's an easy journey, but I can say with certainty that no one I have met or served who has gone through the process has ever regretted it.

Once we do, we stop saying to ourselves, "I'm such an idiot!" Instead, we instinctively use language focusing on the action and outcome, not our identity, such as "Ugh, I made a mistake!" There's a massive difference in how we relate to ourselves when we shift from self-criticism to objectivity. Once you've experienced it, you'll live not in the reflection of the past but in the wonder of who you can become. Life's challenges still appear, but we do not make them any harder on ourselves than necessary. In time, our inner voice stops being our harshest critic and becomes our biggest fan. We find the ability to be at peace with ourselves in our minds for once in our lives. Therein lies true freedom.

Never Let Your Pain Go to Waste

Think about the most significant lessons you've learned in your life. How many of them came from beautiful situations, and how many of them came from pain?

Life will throw us a slew of experiences, some pleasurable and many painful. Emotional health is not about being positive all the time. It's not about making lemonade out of lemons or only acknowledging the silver lining. It's about identifying, processing, and acting upon situations, whether they are pleasurable or painful. It's about navigating painful challenges, processing them, learning from them, and becoming better due to them.

Pain is inevitable in our lives, but suffering is a choice. We must remember that pain has always been (and will always be) our greatest teacher. So, never let your pain go to waste.

CHAPTER NINE

Self-Care

An Easier Way to Support Ourselves

I think there's a perception of self-care that looks like drinking green tea, sitting in bubble baths, or leaving our busy lives behind and chilling on a beach in Costa Rica. Finding your bliss in those environments is not usually difficult, but many of us are too busy to engage in some of those activities or visit such peaceful destinations, at least on a regular basis. That's not to say we can't strive to make those experiences a reality. It's just not always practical, especially if we have businesses to operate or families to raise.

Instead, what if we look at self-care more from the standpoint of the obstacles we can remove from our lives? What if we looked for opportunities to simulate the nature we were built for in our daily lives?

Think back to when we talked about habits. Have you ever used a habit-tracking app to implement a new habit? I have. I figured that the longer I do something, like drinking green juice each day or exercising five times a week, the more habitual it will become. And yes, that is true. But when we're overwhelmed, adding yet another task to our plate, even if it will help us, can feel daunting. When we aren't in a place to grow by addition, we can grow by subtraction.

❝ When we aren't in a place to grow by addition, we can grow by subtraction.

Think about what you might be able to remove from your daily life, something that you tolerate and maybe don't think twice about, that would free up one of your two non-renewable resources: your time and attention.

I had a client, a business owner with a wife and children, who offered to drive his employees to work. They lived somewhat along the way, so they would carpool. That's certainly a kind gesture and beneficial for several reasons; however, there were downsides. For one, it added more time to his commute both ways, especially when, in some cases, he had to wait outside in the car for the employees to get ready. He also lost the only time he had to himself each day. He was no longer able to collect and process his thoughts and feelings. Instead of one hour a day to clear his head while driving, listen to an inspiring podcast, or enjoy the music he loves, he was with two other people in the car. What happened when he came home from a long day? He was short, impatient, and crabby towards his family.

I am not suggesting that we refrain from helping one another. Serving others and creating goodness in the world around us is one of the most fulfilling things we can do in life; however, when that comes at our own expense, we may want to adjust how we serve. Remember our discussion about standards in Chapter Seven?

After my client and I discussed his standards and what he was tolerating, he decided to ask his employees to commute themselves going forward. This gave him much more flexibility with his schedule, and it gave him time to process his thoughts in the car while traveling to work and to mentally leave his business behind while driving home. The result? He's less stressed and overwhelmed than before. And isn't the more emotionally resilient version of himself better for his employees, too?

Where do you tolerate something in your day or week that, when removed, might boost your emotional health? How might taking something off your plate create more time and mental space to decompress, relax, spend time with the people you love, or simply do nothing? Which obstacles are you committed to removing as a form of self-care?

Giving Ourselves Credit

Sometimes, it's hard to give ourselves credit. We give credit to others freely, but when acknowledging our accomplishments, we're not so free to hand out praise.

Is there something wrong with us? Actually, no. We take actions that are consistent with who we believe we are. And if we deal with self-criticism, it's psychologically challenging to give ourselves credit for legitimate progress and accomplishments. Additionally, we live with ourselves every single day. Small, minute changes are almost imperceptible on a day-to-day basis.

Have you ever had the experience of seeing a friend or family member after a long time and having them point out something about you that's changed since they last saw you? Yet, to you, it may not have even registered. That's normal.

The way to overcome this challenge is to track your progress. (Yes, we just talked about doing less as a form of self-care, so I'd recommend adding this in after you've cleared something from your plate). I know tracking progress seems obvious, but do you regularly track what matters to you? Do you track the habits that create optimal emotional health? I was one of those people who absolutely did not journal. I just could not get myself to write consistently, and I was always at a loss for what to write about. To address this, I developed a journaling system that tracks goals, a morning routine, sleep, nutrition, and fitness tracking, and an end-of-day reflection. This system has helped me (and others!) be more intentional about how we live day-to-day life and take action on the things that matter to us. More importantly, it provides a consistent framework for looking back into the past.

Clients have come in after four weeks feeling like nothing has changed, especially regarding mental and emotional markers, but when we review their previous visit, they can see how they have improved. You can do this yourself with a journaling system—all it takes is going back a few weeks to see where you've come from! How are you supposed to know if you're growing or regressing if you don't track your progress? That which gets measured gets done, and your emotional health is no exception. Tracking your progress is a powerful way to give yourself credit.

You can download my journaling system at the reader resources page on my website at drk-arthikramanan.com/reader-resources

Another simple way to practice self-care is to give ourselves credit the same way we might for someone we love.

Do you like receiving money? Most of us do. The reward centers in the brain that are triggered by receiving money are the same as those triggered when we receive compliments from others. What if we applied that same approach to ourselves, reflecting on the effort we put forth and taking pride in how we showed up in a situation that day or how we made it through a tough day and still stayed nice to ourselves?

Many of us tend to feel we deserve a compliment only as a result of achievement, but as we've talked about, setting the achievement bar with high expectations as a means to feel good about ourselves only results in continuing to raise that bar to unattainable levels! We base our compliment worthiness on results rather than effort.

I think many of us, especially the high-achieving perfection-ist types, have sacrificed and worked so hard to get to a certain outcome, only to get to that day and think, "Okay. What next?"

In my Wall Street days, I experienced this in an extreme fashion. For each of the three years prior, we launched a new team and a new service, and I was an instrumental part in mak-ing that happen, so the firm rewarded me. Two senior manag-ers called me into an office, and they passed a handwritten slip across the table. On that slip was my bonus and new salary. My bonus was almost my current salary, and my new salary was nearly double my old one! It was a crazy moment where the value of the dollar in my personal finances drastically shifted for me in an instant.

This was a combination of years of tough 12-14-hour days (and working Saturdays), sacrificing holidays with my family, and draining every ounce of energy I had in my mind and body. I had craved moving up in my career and taking the next step to Vice President for years.

And then, when the moment arrived, as I heard the great news, I internally celebrated for – I kid you not – four seconds. Four seconds! And my immediate next thought was, "What next?"

I couldn't even enjoy this huge, life-changing moment in my career. I couldn't give myself credit and couldn't enjoy the win because it went against my fundamental belief system: that I was simply not good enough for anyone—for me, the firm, my parents, or anyone else. I didn't know it then, but that subjec-tive truth ruled over my unconscious mind and ran my life.

Being driven by "I'm not enough" robs us of the opportuni-ty to truly experience joy in life because the joy comes in the journey. It is in the process; it is not in the result. We've been taught the result is something to celebrate. I say the result is something to strive for, and our actions are what truly count!

Things outside our control often affect our results in life. In contrast, we can control our intentions and actions. What if we focused our compliments on those things within our control?

If this is difficult for you, think about what you might say to your best friend if they were going through a situation you might be experiencing. If you would convey kindness, pride, and congratulations, then allow those exact words to flow freely toward yourself. It may feel uncomfortable at first because, as my clients tell me, they don't want to come off as being arrogant or bragging. As we dig deeper, they discover truth patterns about themselves reinforced by avoidance of self-affirmation. The rational mind considers encouragement to be egotistical, and we use that as an excuse not to give ourselves credit. But there's nothing egotistical about giving ourselves credit for what we actually did or how we showed up!

We can still give ourselves credit for our contribution toward a positive result. You may have graduated from a specific degree program, been promoted, or reached a milestone in your personal or professional life. What's wrong with celebrating that? You can remain humble (a noble thing, for sure!) in that other factors – whether it was the people around us or even a little bit of good fortune – allowed us to create that outcome.

The reality is that humility and giving yourself credit can go hand in hand because humility just means that you understand that forces and factors outside yourself allow you to get there. Nothing happens consistently without outside influence. So, acknowledging others who have allowed you to do what you deserve credit for embraces humility as you give yourself credit.

Growing up, many of us never witnessed those around us modeling self-compassion or giving themselves credit. As a result, we developed this sense that it's normal not to give ourselves credit and to dismiss our efforts and results. When you practice the art of giving yourself credit with humility, not only do you honor and compliment the others around you who support your efforts, but you show them how to be kinder to themselves along the way.

When you struggle to give yourself credit or celebrate your wins, you want to dig deeper into it. Not from a place of judgment but from a place of curiosity. What would be untrue of yourself if you were to take credit? Giving ourselves credit is a simple, free, and highly effective way of practicing self-care. What will you commit to giving yourself credit for more often?

Giving Ourselves Grace

How do you give yourself grace when you try your best, and it doesn't work out? It's easy to beat ourselves up when things don't go well. But hey! You made the best choice with the information you had at the time. Sometimes, those strategic decisions just go against you.

Think about it. If you have a 75% chance your decision will succeed, there's a 25% chance it will fail. If you only get one opportunity, one at-bat, there is still a pretty sizable chance that it will backfire. If it does, is it fair to beat yourself up?

Giving ourselves grace relates to the expectations and standards discussed in Chapter Six. When we cannot give ourselves grace, our expectations of ourselves are too high, and our standards are too low. If you expect the world of yourself and don't reach that milestone, you are hard on yourself. Your standards are too low when you tolerate that negative self-talk!

Flip that to the framework for joy. It tells you to lower your expectations once again and raise your standards. Now, you might think, "Okay, you know what? I tried this, but it went against me, and that's fine. I can give myself some grace for it. But I will not use this as an opportunity to beat myself up. I'm going to use this as an opportunity to grow."

That is giving yourself grace, which is the same as giving yourself credit. If you can't give yourself credit, it's because your expectations of yourself are through the roof. I've been there! I get it. And it's not healthy. It's not helpful. Being graceful in the process and the journey is a core component of an emotionally healthy life. That is raising your standards. And that will make it easier to give yourself credit and grace.

When we lower our expectations of ourselves and raise our standards in how we treat ourselves, we shift from beating ourselves up (and likely making some disempowering self "truth" true) to using the situation as an opportunity to learn and grow.

Celebrate You!

You may ask yourself, "How can I recognize and congratulate my small wins?" The simple answer is to ask yourself: If this were your best friend, would you recognize and congratulate them for the small win? If your friend were going through the same situation and you would congratulate them, then the same applies to you. If your best friend deserves a celebration, so do you!

Sometimes, we don't even recognize the extraordinary things we do daily. It could be your ability to stay calm and objective when your kids drive you up a wall. Maybe you can listen to a co-worker who's having a difficult day, even when you're struggling inside. Perhaps it's your ability to get up and work out every morning. That might just be something that you see as part of your identity, and it's not a big deal, but for a lot of people in the world, that's a huge deal!

It's important to be able to separate your subjective reality from objective reality. What seems ordinary to you may be extraordinary to someone else. And if it is, it's worth acknowledging and celebrating! You can choose to be grateful for that aspect of who you are and the circumstances that led there. It's so easy for us to focus on all the things that we're not and ignore the things we are.

Surround yourself with other growth seekers, for when you are with other people who recognize and congratulate you on your small wins, as well as their own, it becomes easier for you to do the same. You can learn more about surrounding yourself with growth seekers as a member of my Insiders Club.

I begin every session in my group workshops by asking participants to share one win. It doesn't even have to be about the program topic. What is something that happened this week that you're proud of? It could be a huge win, or it could be, "You know what? I was feeling crappy, but I showed up today." That is a great win! It demonstrates that we are willing to do something despite not feeling like it.

At the start of every session, my personal trainer asks me, "How are we feeling?" Sometimes, I respond, "Today, I'm just showing up," and that's my win.

Acknowledging who we are and surrounding ourselves with people who can help us in our weak areas helps us become better. That is how we become better together. When you're around other growth-seeking individuals who do the same thing, it becomes easier to acknowledge, recognize, and congratulate yourself on the small wins. The celebrations follow. We become more similar to those we surround ourselves with, so be intentional and choose wisely.

Why Self-Care Might Be Challenging

Let's acknowledge and set aside the two most common reasons self-care activities may be challenging. First, time may be limited. Perhaps you're a busy parent, corporate professional, business owner, community leader, or any combination thereof. We all have a limited amount of time each day, and there may be little time to prioritize taking care of ourselves.

Another reason is money. Many of the activities we might want to engage in cost money, and if that's limited, self-care may suffer. However, what stops us from sitting outside in the sun and connecting with ourselves for a brief moment while enjoying our coffee instead of being on our phones?

Our past may influence our present more than we realize. We need to understand our truths about ourselves and what we think is expected of us. If, for instance, we've come to believe that we're undeserving of love, that others always come first, or it's more important to be liked by others than honor our own needs, self-care becomes increasingly difficult. We may know we want and need it, but when we experience any sign of resistance, we default to putting everything else ahead of our needs.

The human mind prioritizes present-day pain avoidance and pleasure-seeking. It goes against our nature to take action now for a gain we may or may not see in the future, which is why it's difficult for many people to prioritize healthy habits today to prevent chronic disease tomorrow or invest even a small amount in life insurance or an index fund now for future financial stability.

❚❚ We don't see it to believe it. We believe it to see it.

Today, it feels more important to prioritize others over ourselves. And that's okay! There will be moments when we put our needs and plans aside to help someone in need. That's among the most beautiful aspects of us as human beings, and we never want to lose that. However, if we zoom out and look at the following year, five years, ten years, or twenty years, do we want to be able to make a positive impact in the lives of those around us in the future, as well? If so, what do we need to do today to ensure that our commitment to others is sustainable and doesn't come at the expense of our longevity?

I invite you to zoom out and consider how helpful you can be to those around you if you reach burnout, fall ill, or want to throw your hands in the air and walk away. A small investment in self-care now will allow you to be the best version of yourself and serve everyone you love for years to come.

CHAPTER 10

A New Perspective

How to Practice Emotionally Healthy Communication

Have you ever been in an argument with a loved one that goes back and forth, where neither of you is truly able to listen and process the other's feelings? Have you had the experience of a long argument where one line gets taken out of context, and the other person doesn't let that point go? The situation goes something like, "I just spent an hour explaining, and that one sentence is what you want to focus on?!"

Think about the experience of using a camera and choosing between different zoom levels. Standard lenses generally give you the perspective of the human eye, give or take. These are photos in which the content looks in proportion to the actual object or space.

Your wide-angle lens gives a broad perspective of left and right, up and down, stretching beyond the standard human field of view to provide you with more to see in a constrained photograph. This often makes spaces look more vast and wide-open than they are. Perhaps you've had that experience when looking at real estate photos, and when you visit the house, the room looks much smaller than it does in the pictures.

In contrast, telephoto lenses provide a zoomed-in view of your surroundings. These are useful in nature photography to get a close-up view of an animal far away. Though they serve their purpose, telephoto lenses might not be the best for showing the perspective of surrounding areas because of their limited focal view.

Now, consider our busy lives as we focus on getting through the day at work and caring for our families and ourselves as best as we can. All that matters is right here and right now.

In the photography analogy, which lens represents our perspective each day? It's probably the telephoto lens. We zoom in, focus, and see many details about a small space. At that moment, we lack a perspective of the greater situation. When we communicate with others, we easily zoom in on the perspective we see and build our vision of reality around an image without a broader perspective. When we do, we're constantly scanning the world around us, looking for evidence that fits the truth we've formed around our zoomed-in view. Any other evidence gets rejected automatically, many times without our knowing. Therefore, the lens we use to examine ourselves and the world determines our reality. At this point, we don't see it to believe it. We believe it to see it.

❝❝ **We don't see it to believe it. We believe it to see it.**

Communication Starts From Within
Companies contact me to speak to their teams on various topics related to emotional health. When I talk to them about their pain points, a common one is communication: "We have a communication problem. It's like people here sometimes speak different languages."

I smile any time I hear that, for how can we master communication with another person until we understand our own minds? How often have we experienced misunderstandings in a relationship, and the other person says something like, "I shouldn't have to tell you. You should know!"? If we are not incredibly clear on identifying and processing how we ourselves feel, how can we expect someone else to read our minds? Communication starts with self-mastery, and you can begin that journey using some of the frameworks discussed in this book.

Once we develop an understanding of our own mind, we can do two things.

First, we can convey how we feel to another person and give them a game plan for how to talk to us in a similar situation in the future. Second, and even more importantly, we can recognize that the other person is viewing the situation in question (and their life in general) through their own lens. Only when we train ourselves to see things through a different lens—from another perspective—can we truly communicate with others.

When we own this philosophy, we put the onus on ourselves to know our own minds and actively look through an alternate lens to understand where the other person is coming from.

Our Mind's Influence on Perspective: The Amygdala Hijack
Think of a time when you argued with someone and defended your position in an effort to prove you were right. Perhaps you were unable to think clearly at that moment, yet later, when cooler heads prevailed, you were able to be more objective with what happened. Maybe you regretted how you handled things.

If this happens often, we might wonder, "What is wrong with me? Why do I keep doing this?" Nothing is wrong with you! We're designed this way. What you experience when you are triggered, unable to think clearly, and act purely out of emotion is called the Amygdala Hijack.

Psychotherapist Danial Goleman coined the term "Amygdala Hijack" to describe a sudden, intense emotional reaction that feels overwhelming and disproportionate to the actual situation.

Let's first explain a few brain structures and how they function, once again remembering that we were designed for nature, not this modern world.

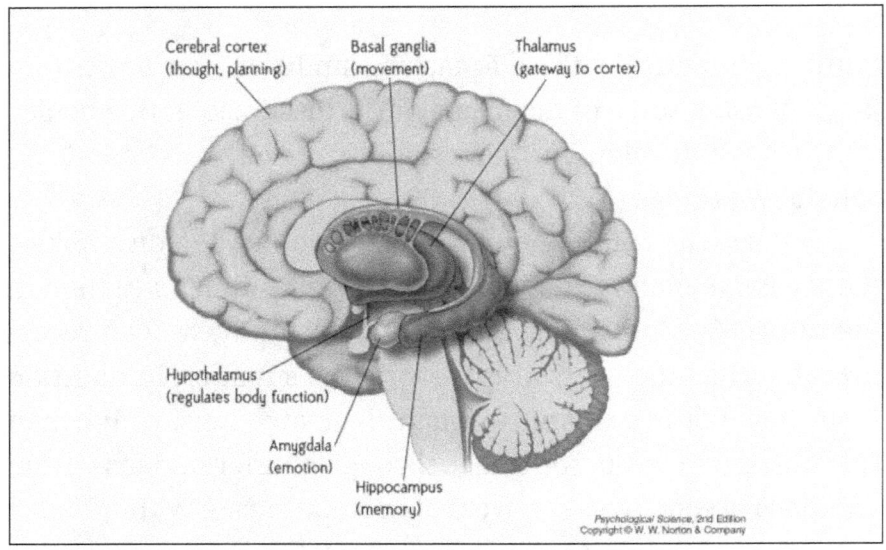

When we receive a stimulus (sensory information like sight, sound, etc), the signals route to the thalamus, the brain's sensory relay station. The thalamus then routes the information to the cortex and the amygdala.

The cortex is where we process rational thought, processing information more slowly and methodically, as it's in charge of decision-making.

The amygdala is part of the limbic system, a set of structures we share with other animals. It is in charge of emotions and fear and is the primary safety assessor of our nervous system. The amygdala is also in contact with the hippocampus, which contains a library of past threats stored in long-term memory. The amygdala is a fast-acting structure that scans the environment for threats to keep us safe.

Think back to our phone call and pattern recognition from chapter three. Your ears hear the sound waves emanating from the ringing phone, and your eyes then receive a signal from the light patterns on your phone's screen.

Let's say this call is from someone you like. The light signal travels down the optic nerve. Your thalamus routes this information to your cortex and your amygdala. Your amygdala asks the hippocampus if this is a threat; the hippocampus essentially says "no." The amygdala moves on, and your slower-acting cortex looks at the caller ID, so you decide to pick up the phone.

Now, let's say you don't want to talk with the person calling. The same process unfolds, but this time, the hippocampus tells the amygdala, "Yes, this person is a threat!" The amygdala reacts by signaling to the cortex to abort function. We're in danger! Our emotional reaction is often out of proportion to the situation at hand because we may have a history of emotional memories fueling this exaggerated response.

The amygdala sends signals to flood the body with stress hormones like epinephrine and cortisol, and at this point, we're in a fight-flight-freeze response. Rational thought can't fully occur, as the cortex was instructed to take a back seat to the emergency.

This very situation can happen when we communicate with others. If they say something that triggers us, it may send us into amygdala hijack. At this point, we often feel a sense of "tunnel vision" and an intense desire to feel right, to win the argument. We rarely mean what we say in the heat of the moment, and often, memory is impaired during amygdala hijack, so we may not even remember what we said. The problem is, the other person can't un-hear what we say. You can't put the toothpaste back in the tube.

The average person needs around 20 minutes to recover from an amygdala hijack in an average situation, so it's best to avoid discussing the issue in the heat of the moment. Instead, say, "I'm angry right now. We'll talk later." Then, walk away. Learn to pause before reacting. Understanding our subjective truths and the triggers that drive our behaviors allows us to realize that the situations we face don't always directly correlate with those that have occurred in the past.

After both of you have processed your emotions, it's critical to discuss what happened, how you each felt, and, most importantly, what you can learn from this experience and how to prevent it in the future. The ability to step away from a heated argument when one or both of you are experiencing an amygdala hijack is a vital component of emotionally healthy communication. Though we may each treat our own perspective as reality, it's always important to remember that each of our realities is subjective.

It takes energy and effort to see things from a different perspective, and most people don't do that because they were designed for nature. In nature, energy is scarce, and we don't want to waste excess energy. But that doesn't mean we can't. It just takes an active approach and a human desire to improve a situation.

Another person's lens is determined by their upbringing, their experiences in life, and all the influences they've experienced to the present day. We inherit truth patterns from our parents, generations before us, and our culture and society. We even carry forward epigenetic traits from ancestors based on their experiences. (Epigenetics refers to changes in gene expression that can be passed on from one generation to another. The genes coded may be the same, but epigenetics refers to which genes are effectively activated or not activated.) Overall, we are dealt a certain hand in life. It's a unique hand that no other human in history has experienced. You are unique, as is everyone around you.

Let's examine a character, Matt. Maybe Matt's parents divorced when he was young, which affected his self-worth. Perhaps Matt was bullied in school, further damaging his self-confidence. Later in life, he endured a rough breakup, job loss, and other situations that continued to wear on his sense of self.

To adapt to these life circumstances, Matt might have developed a powerful sensitivity and ability to empathize with others, as he never wants others to feel hurt the way he did growing up. Or he may have developed a sense of false bravado and narcissistic tendencies to compensate for not feeling good about himself. Either way, the root cause of life experiences might be similar.

How might we have learned to see ourselves if we had had Matt's entire life? We may have done things differently, but if we base that on our view, we need to remember that who we currently are is an evolution of the person who went through the conditions, tragedies, and triumphs of our lives, not Matt's. When we attempt to understand how someone thinks, we can glimpse the truths they live by and seek to understand rather than blame them. We can then step back and ask ourselves, "How can we make this conversation productive? What is in our long-term best interest, both individually and together?"

If you were a business owner or corporate manager, and Matt was your employee, dismissing him as difficult to work with might be easy. Or, you could seek to understand where he's coming from and explore what conditions allow him to perform at his best. You could communicate with him in a manner he prefers – for example, direct and to the point, or softer and less direct. We can adapt our communication to create the best possible outcome by seeking to understand.

Being a great communicator is not about what you say or how you say it. It's about what the other person hears. You can give the most outstanding presentation, make the greatest case, and deliver excellent feedback. Still, if it doesn't land as you intended for your audience, your communication will not have the desired effect. Maybe it has no impact or even has an opposite or detrimental effect.

Three Types of Communication

It's essential to know three types of communication.

The first is verbal. Verbal communication is written language that can be communicated through a text message, an email, a social media post, or a billboard along the highway. Verbal communication has the advantage of being easily re-readable and referenced later. However, if you've ever sent a text message that got wildly misinterpreted, you've experienced the limitations of verbal communication. There is limited context, no tone of voice, no visual indicators of the other person's intentions, and no physical presence to "feel" out a situation.

Next, we have vocal communication. We receive spoken language as the words spoken to us, along with tone. We can communicate vocally through phone calls and audio messages. A step up from verbal communication, vocal communication can better convey a thought or feeling, but it still lacks the visual or physical element.

Visual communication involves seeing a person's face as they speak. We can achieve this through recorded videos on social media, video calls, and in-person conversations. This third form of communication allows us to hear and interpret spoken language, accounting for auditory and visual cues indicating the other person's meaning.

Imagine the word "Oh." Say, "Oh" out loud the way you would if you just heard good news. Now say, "Oh," like you just heard terrible news. Next, say, "Oh," to convey frustration. Now, say, "Oh," to express your surprise.

Notice how one word can mean so many different things? Suppose someone expresses "Oh" in the form of being surprised. Much is lost if all you see is "Oh" in verbal communication. If you hear "Oh," you have more of an idea. If you see someone while hearing them say, "Oh," you can sometimes interpret the degree to which they were surprised.

There is another level of communication, though. It's the ability to fully set your inner thoughts aside, be completely present with the other person, and listen without concurrently assessing. It takes practice, but once you master it, you'll find that people develop trust in you, and you'll have a more positive influence on others.

Ideally, the more critical the conversation, the more you want a conversation that utilizes visual communication, either a video call or in-person. In-person communication allows us to fully engage mirror neurons in charge of firing when we observe an action performed by another, thereby allowing us to "mirror" the other participant's behavior. While mirror neurons appear to fire in deeply immersive online experiences, like virtual reality (VR) and augmented reality (AR), their effectiveness still only mimics what we experience in face-to-face interactions. Mirror neurons play a vital role in empathy. As stated earlier, communication occurs much more effectively when we seek to understand someone's point of view rather than talking at them. For emotionally healthy communication, strive to engage in visual communication, ideally in person, for the most vital of conversations.

Second-Order Thinking

To practice emotionally healthy communication, utilize second-order thinking. First-order thinking is simplistic and surface-level. It considers only the present moment and ignores any long-term implications, whereas second-order thinking considers the ripple effect and possible consequences of our actions.

Let's say your friend Megan didn't invite you to a party. You might feel neglected, hurt, and sad. You might look at past interactions with her and say, "She's always playing favorites." To counteract this, you confront her and say, "Next time, I'd love to get an invite." That's the first-order thinking approach.

But what might happen next? She might invite you out of obligation, likely making up a story about you being dramatic. Perhaps she doesn't ask you out of principle, and you continue feeling left out. Either way, the desired result of wanting to be closer to Megan is left unfulfilled.

Instead of utilizing that first-order thinking approach, what if we looked at things more objectively? If we did, we might consider that she had a reason for not inviting us. There may have been space constraints. Maybe she knew you were busy with some challenging personal matters and didn't want you to feel compelled to attend. Maybe she simply made a mistake and forgot. Or perhaps she is being spiteful. We don't know, so utilizing second-order thinking, if you want to get closer to Megan as your friend, what might that look like? Perhaps you could ask her to lunch, just you and her, or invite her to a shared activity you enjoy doing together to spend quality time and catch up. What if she agrees to meet you for lunch, and during that time, you share a good laugh and catch up on life? Maybe the topic of the party comes up, and she explains her thinking, or she doesn't (let's say it was due to headcount constraints), but she keeps you in mind for future occasions because you're both feeling more connected. That's second-order thinking.

You can apply this in the workplace, too. Let's say you're a business owner, and your employee Ben drops the ball on following up with an important client proposal. First-order thinking might look like showing your frustration towards him for not following through, but second-order thinking would involve processing your emotions first and then approaching him to ask about the follow-up.

If you take the first-order thinking approach and harshly

micromanage Ben, voicing your frustration, you might lose his trust. Suppose Ben is a sensitive individual who likes to be given direction but likes the feeling of coming up with solutions on his own. In that case, you may get immediate satisfaction in getting the job done the way you want, but what will the effect be later? Generally, the moment that person has a new job opportunity, they're out the door, and you just lost a talented person. So, you always want to think about the outcome you want before you say anything.

What if, instead of taking out your frustration on Ben, you ask him, "How can I best support you for proposals like this in the future?" In that scenario, you could learn the actual cause for Ben not calling the client. Maybe after a few similar situations and questions, you realize Ben's skill set is more in people skills and influence and less in the details and task follow-ups, so you ask a teammate, Emily, who is proficient with details and task execution, to help Ben with proposals going forward.

By asking the right questions, starting with the desired result, and working backward, you can employ second-order thinking, leverage Ben's strengths, and give Emily a role she enjoys.

To utilize second-order thinking, consider the effects of each possible course of action. Remember your desired result, and use the "if-then" approach for each possible course of action to determine how you can get closest to that end.

Understand Who You're Talking To

There are various ways of learning to speak with someone personally, professionally, in a group, or an organization.

One method would be DISC or some other assessment to understand how people communicate so you can say things in a way that lands for them. For instance, let's say we were using the DISC model. You're talking to somebody who exhibits a "High D," or Dominance, which means they are a fast-moving, task-oriented person. You could simply say, "Okay, I need this done this way." They'll say, "Got it," and complete the task.

Meanwhile, suppose you wanted to communicate with a "High C" (Conscientiousness) individual who's still task-oriented but a little bit slower moving and more analytical. In that case, you might want to give that person an opportunity to devise their own solution. You might say, "This is the problem, and we need a solution. Here's what I'm thinking, but I'd love to know how you would solve this problem, too." Then, you will need to give this person more time so they can work their way through the issue and come up with a great solution.

Knowing who you're talking to goes beyond understanding their personality or motivations. It requires developing a sense of that person's emotions. Perhaps they are exhibiting signs of stress, something is going on in their personal life, or they're not feeling well, or maybe they just didn't sleep well last night. You still want to communicate with them. You still want to get this project in their hands, but as you walk up, you sense that something's off. In that case, perhaps your first question is, "Hey, I came with a question, but how are you feeling?" You check in with the person first and see how they're feeling because if you deliver your intended message to this person in the usual way that works, but their state isn't their normal one, you may not get the desired effect of your communication. However, you can adjust how you deliver that information based on the present circumstances.

Can you put the person receiving your message at the center? Are they the hero of their own journey? Or are you barking orders, making yourself the focal point?

Ultimately, when we can empower our conversation partners or our team in the way they want and then slightly push them outside their comfort zone to grow, they derive a sense of purpose and an intrinsic desire to be productive and helpful. This is critical for emotionally healthy communication.

Check out the worksheet for emotionally healthy communication on my website at <u>drk-arthikramanan.com/reader-resources</u>

Healthy Communication Takes Timing

Remember, the one rule I have for emotionally healthy communication is this: Being a great communicator is not about what you say or how you say it. It's about what the other person hears.

> ❝ **Being a great communicator is not about what you say or how you say it. It's about what the other person hears.**

Granted, there's a lot that's outside your control. You don't know what this person is going through that day or whether your comment will set them off, but a big part of emotionally healthy communication is sensing how that other person is feeling before we engage. Sometimes, the best way to communicate is to hold off until later.

Imagine you and your romantic partner are arguing. Something comes up, and one of you is triggered, and then both of you are triggered. Think of the words exchanged at that time. They are not helpful, productive, or going to lead anywhere, and you may say things you regret later. So sometimes, emotionally healthy communication is knowing when not to have the conversation or when to have it later.

All we can do is do our best. When we make communication mistakes, taking responsibility for our actions and how they may have affected the other person and seeking to find out how we can improve their situation goes a long way toward healing relationships and creating everlasting bonds with the people closest to us.

The so-called Platinum Rule applies in communication, as well. Treat others how they want to be treated.

CHAPTER 11

The 5 Pillars Of Emotional Health

The 5 Pillars in Practice

In this chapter, we'll discuss my favorite practical approaches to improving your emotional health. I encourage you to consider implementing them over time, though it may be easier to implement one at a time. We'll start with some simple frameworks that have an immediate impact, and work our way to some frameworks that have an additive effect when practiced regularly.

Do What Makes You Feel Alive!
What are some of the things you enjoy doing for no particular reason? These might be activities you have enjoyed since childhood, or you may have picked them up along the way in life. Think of the small things that put a smile on your face. Maybe it's a hobby you're good at or one you don't think you're good at, but you enjoy it nonetheless! What are the activities that disconnect your mind from the major tasks at hand, those that, when you engage, you come away feeling lighter, more energetic, and just plain happier?

Surprisingly, the busier we get, the less time we make for "our things." The more stressed and overwhelmed we feel, the more we think we have to take care of the tasks at hand before we can engage in the activities that make us feel most alive.

We treat these activities as optional, and that's okay. But consider this: Would being more energized, present, and focused allow you to better manage the challenges that arise in your life?

107

Try it out. Take some time today (or maybe even right now) to go do something you enjoy, your 'things' you don't have to justify to anyone. Maybe it's singing, going to the gym for a workout, or a walk outside. Perhaps it's playing a musical instrument, preparing a nice dish, or invoking your creativity through artwork.

When we're children, we don't need an excuse to play. It's part of who we are. I believe we never truly outgrow the desire to play as adults; we just place guardrails on ourselves because of what we think is expected of us. Over time, that wears us down and eats into who we truly are.

'Your Things' To Do Now - *The 5 Pillars in Practice*
- ❑ Make a list of things you enjoy doing for no good reason, the things that make you feel alive.
- ❑ Create a plan for when and how many times you will do that activity this week.
- ❑ Let me know how this strategy worked for you by emailing me at hello@drkarthikramanan.com

These and all the Action Items from this chapter are included as a checklist in the workbook found on the reader resources page of my website at drkarthikramanan.com/reader-resources

Identify the Root Cause of Human Needs
There are many models of human needs, perhaps the most well-known being Maslow's Hierarchy of Needs. Other models include ERG Theory, McClelland's Acquired Needs Theory, and others. I like to focus on four areas of human needs for my clients: stability, belonging, growth, and purpose.

Stability

Stability includes the roof over our heads, the food to nourish us, the people we count on, the employment that provides us income, the absence of significant debt, and other basic needs that allow us to feel safe. Remember, we were built for nature, so the very things we would need to survive in nature – shelter, food, our families/tribes, safety – are vital to feeling a sense of stability. In our modern world, at least to a certain baseline, money equates to safety since it is the currency by which we can acquire other needs like food and shelter.

When we lose our jobs, our relationships fall apart, or money is tight, we lack stability. At that point, the need for stability prevails over any other need.

Belonging

Belonging is our need to feel a part of a group. Think about the human being in nature. In the animal kingdom, are we the strongest? Fastest? Definitely not! Our strength in survival comes from being a part of a community. This is why our need to fit in is so strong in day-to-day life. Whether in high school trying to navigate our social groups or adults trying to figure out who "our people" are, our instinct dictates a need to feel like we belong. We have a primal need to belong to our families, communities, workplaces, and online groups. In nature, being cast out significantly affects our survivability. In modern life, it impacts our emotional health.

When we feel isolated from others, it becomes easier to spiral into our own thoughts, bridging the information gap about why we're lonely. In that absence of belonging, we adapt in one way or another: through addictions, overachieving to prove others wrong, or even hating on others to pull them down.

Creating a positive sense of belonging for another person is as simple as saying, "Hello!" or complimenting a stranger. The more we spread small doses of kindness, the better we can influence each other's emotional health, and the more we'll feel like we belong to ourselves and within the communities around us.

> ❚❚ **The more we create a positive sense of belonging for others, the more we feel we belong.**

Growth

Growth is the need to be more today than we were yesterday. This isn't necessarily a biological need, at least for adults, because we're fully optimized to conserve energy. Generally, people don't like too much change, nor are we eager to change ourselves. It takes metabolic energy. But the human spirit, like a child living in wonder, constantly seeks growth. Much like in nature and business, if we're not growing and evolving to adapt to the changes around us, we're slowly dying.

But growing doesn't have to be scary. It can be as simple as living slightly outside our comfort zone. Perhaps you're learning to play the guitar, and after a great deal of practice, you can play your favorite music. Being satisfied here is quite okay! There's nothing wrong with that. But what if a part of you enjoyed the feeling of growing in this skill? Stretching beyond your comfort zone to expand who you are allows you to feel the satisfaction that comes from growth.

By contrast, have you ever felt stuck in life? Have you ever felt like every day is like the day before, and you don't feel like you're moving forward? That's what a lack of growth feels like. Focus on growing, and as you do, your emotional health improves.

Purpose

Purpose might be the hardest thing to solidify, but once you do, life is never the same! Philosophers have been asking the questions, "Who am I?" and "Why am I here?" in some form for thousands of years worldwide. When humans reached a certain level of self-awareness and recognized the vastness of the world around them, they naturally began to question their role within it—their purpose.

Without purpose, it's hard to get up on those days when we feel we can't push forward. Without purpose, we don't have a guiding light to decide which choices to make and which to avoid. Without purpose, we question ourselves and allow the perceived expectations of others to dictate our actions.

People often ask me, "Dr. K, how do I find my purpose?" There isn't a simple formula for finding it, but I'll share some ways it can happen. One, it may just become evident to you one day, out of nowhere. Two, it might require exploring what resonates with you and what does not. Or three—and this is my journey—we own our past, learn from our pain, and serve others with the lessons learned.

After several years of being around one another, a fellow doctor and I finally sat down for a real get-to-know-you conversation. We talked about business for a while, and then he asked me a question that took me by surprise: "What are your personal goals?"

I froze, stumbled on my words, and couldn't come up with a real answer for him. Only later did it hit me—my business goals are my personal goals. My goal is to serve as many people as I possibly can, helping them move from overwhelm, burnout, self-criticism, and struggle into a state of emotional health, growth, and purpose. This is what I was put on Earth to do.

I have bad days, too. I have the days where I struggle to focus, make mistakes, and feel defeated. But strong emotional health means we reduce the severity and duration of those moments, and we're soon back on track. And what is that track? Purpose.

Human Needs in Action

When you're not feeling great, ask yourself which human need requires attention: stability, belonging, growth, or purpose. It can be more than one at a time, and looking at our human needs allows us to get to the root cause.

For example, if it's a stability problem due to money, consider doing one of 'your things' that energizes you, and then look at the numbers. Maybe ask for support from someone who can help you navigate and solve the problem. Then take action!

If it's an absence of belonging, what can you do to create a little connection with another person today? Perhaps it's going to a coffee shop and giving someone an unconditional compliment. Or maybe it's calling that friend you haven't spoken to in a while.

If you lack growth, take one step toward improving yourself in an area of interest. You don't become an expert overnight, but the satisfaction of incremental improvement is a powerful fuel for emotional well-being.

If all those areas are solid and you lack a sense of purpose, go out and explore ways to serve others. Maybe it's volunteering or getting involved with a not-for-profit organization you're passionate about. Perhaps it's building a business around the lessons learned from your past experiences that you can now use to serve others.

Human Needs Action Items - *Pillars in Practice:*

❑ Rate your satisfaction with each of the four human needs on a scale of 1 to 10, with 10 being completely fulfilled.

❑ Which areas need improvement?

❑ Now, create a specific plan for how you're going to make that need better.

These and all the Action Items from this chapter are included as a checklist in the workbook found on the reader resources page of my website at drkarthikramanan.com/reader-resources

Your Morning "Me Time"

Imagine you're winding down for the day. You set the alarm on your phone for your wake-up time. You lie in bed as you scroll through social media for an extra half hour when you could have been sleeping. (Yes, I have done this many times myself).

You put the phone on your nightstand and go to sleep. Somewhere in the middle of the night, you wake up and go to the bathroom. When you come back, what do you do? Of course, you check your phone. After all, someone might have texted at 2:30 AM, right?

After struggling to fall back asleep, the alarm eventually jars you awake. You desperately reach over to turn off the glaring sound, and what happens next? Your phone is in your hand, so naturally, it's time to check notifications, texts, social media, and emails. A half-hour goes by and your feet haven't even touched the floor. In this moment, you've given up control of your entire day.

Let's dive into human biology for a minute. Again, we're made for nature. That includes the natural rising and setting of the sun and the resulting exposure to the light frequencies. White lights from our electronic devices and some lamps late in the evening create a dysregulation effect on our circadian rhythm (body clock) by exposing us to light frequencies consistent with daytime sunlight. When we look at our phones late at night, we expose our eyes to these frequencies, impacting melatonin (the stay-asleep hormone) and cortisol (the alertness hormone). Additionally, we're activating our minds to process the day's events when we wind down for sleep.

Around thirty minutes after waking up in the morning, our cortisol levels reach the peak of the day. Remember, cortisol is a stress hormone, an alertness hormone. Why, in nature, would we need it to peak after waking up? To find food! We've been fasting during the hours of sleep, and our cortisol rises so we can find food to nourish ourselves.

While we gather ourselves during the first 30 minutes after waking, as cortisol rises, we can make a massive difference in our day by starting it on our terms. Your notifications are someone else's agenda for you. And when we heed that agenda before checking in on ourselves first, we're in reaction mode from there on.

By contrast, starting your day on your terms allows you to connect with yourself, set your day in motion, and create emotional resilience for the challenges that may arise.

So here's what you do. Put your phone in another room at night to charge. Get yourself one of those old-school alarm clocks, or if you want to be fancy, you can buy a sunrise light alarm clock (I love mine). If you need to be able to hear the phone for late-night emergencies, you can charge the phone across the room. The point is to have it away from you so you're not tempted to touch it before bed, in the middle of the night, or after waking up.

Create a morning routine that inspires you! Maybe you've wanted to meditate daily, pray more regularly, journal, or spend time outside. Make sure to include something you love after you awaken and freshen up. This might also be a chance to do one of 'your things,' the things that make you feel alive. You can even double up, for instance, by journaling while sitting outside.

Connecting with ourselves each morning as part of our

morning routine allows us to learn how to respond more proactively to the world around us. By regularly applying this practice, we rehearse seeing our environments and ourselves more objectively.

I recommend getting some sunlight exposure in the morning, as that can help set your circadian rhythm for the day. In fact, a great night's sleep starts the morning before.

Morning Me Time Action Items - *Pillars in Practice:*
- ❑ Put your phone in another room at night
- ❑ Create a morning routine that inspires you
- ❑ Consider using the Dr. K Journal for journaling prompts and habit tracking for your emotional health - go to <u>drkjournal.com</u>

These and all the Action Items from this chapter are included as a checklist in the workbook found on the reader resources page of my website at <u>drkarthikramanan.com/reader-resources</u>

Visualization

What's more challenging, facing a brand new situation or facing a situation you've been in before? Naturally, if we've experienced something before, handling it a second time is easier. Why is that? Please note that while this is a highly simplified explanation, the evidence strongly suggests that when we experience an event, a common "core" brain network is activated. We construct spatial contexts (the "scene" of the event), fill in details like people and objects that were a part of that event, and process our subjective experience of that event. These pathways are utilized while experiencing an event and while recalling a memory.

It's safe to say that the past affects us. We experience the past through memories. What if we could use a neural pathway similar to memories to drive a future outcome? We can! This is visualization.

Functional MRI studies indicate that a shared network is engaged while remembering past happenings and imagining or simulating future events. The ability to construct a scene involving the part of the brain known as the hippocampus is heavily involved in both processes, as our brains effectively paint a picture of the events similarly. Even when the brain uses other areas to process fictitious experiences, it appears that this common core memory network is engaged, perhaps indicating that even as we're considering new possibilities, we're filtering through the same network that remembers past experiences.

Does imagining or visualizing a future occurrence help us improve our focus, better handle it, or increase our performance?

Guided imagery and visualization enhance attention and cognitive performance and reduce stress. They activate similar brain regions as physical practice, creating neural pathways and "muscle memory" (though nothing replicates the effectiveness of physical practice). Additionally, performance anxiety is reduced, and mental readiness increases. Some evidence indicates that sports performance can improve by incorporating visualization, physical training, and repetition. In a study examining martial artists, participants who combined visualization and motivational self-talk significantly reduced their reaction times, some by as much as 20%.

So, what does this all mean for us? Let's zoom out. Our past affects our present, and our memories influence how we show up and take action today. But if memory and visualization are neurologically similar processes, why don't we create "memories" of a future we desire and live into that vision today? That's visualization!

In medical school, I would visualize every major exam. I would picture myself amping up before entering the room. I would know in which specific room the exam was taking place, and if I hadn't been to that room before, I would visit the space ahead of time to construct the scene in my mind. I would visualize going into the room and sitting down at a desk. I would picture myself breathing and staying calm as someone handed out the exam. I would visualize going through the questions, feeling a sense of confidence build as I filled out each answer. Then, I would add a curveball because we all know those unforeseen events happen in life! I would imagine coming across a question that stumped me. I'd picture skipping it to come back later but then not knowing the answer to the next one. I envisioned feeling that bit of overwhelm creeping in, then visualized breathing through it while practicing resilience. I would then play out the movie in my head and finish the rest of the test, returning to those questions and confidently answering them. I would picture turning in the exam and walking out, knowing I did well.

You can visualize both the long-term outcomes you desire in your life and the events of that day. As with everything, visualization is a practice; the more you do it, the more effective it becomes.

For more on visualization, you can visit chapter three or my seven-day guided visualization program on the reader resource page of my website: drkarthikramanan.com/reader-resources.

Visualization Action Item - Pillars in Practice:
As part of your next morning routine, sit down and visualize an upcoming event in which you need to do well. Visualize the space, the surrounding details, and your internal feelings. Picture everything going according to plan. Imagine feeling pow-

erful and in charge. Then, visualize something going wrong. Play out how you process and navigate that situation in your mind and recover beautifully. Then, visualize completing the event successfully.

These and all the Action Items from this chapter are included as a checklist in the workbook found on the reader resources page of my website at drkarthikramanan.com/reader-resources

I Am / I Am Not

This next practice ties in with the Truth Cycle. If you remember the model from Chapter Three, human beings use their senses to detect patterns and construct a story around them. When we see that story play out, we take the moral of the story and turn it into a belief. When we see that belief play out in life many times, it becomes our truth. This truth becomes the lens through which we see the world. Understanding this lens is vital to understanding our patterns and behaviors.

One practical way to understand our truths is to examine the language we use, especially around the words "I am" and "I am not." These are statements of identity, ones we take to be the truth about ourselves. The most powerful words we use come after the words "I am."

> ❝ **The most powerful words we use come after the words "I am."**

I Am / I Am Not Action Items - *Pillars in Practice:*
- ❑ Set aside 15-30 minutes. Take out a sheet of paper and on one side write "I am ___" and on the other side write "I am not ___"

❑ Take some time to brainstorm the words you use toward yourself or believe about yourself. Do not edit as you brainstorm; just let the pen do the thinking. These can be empowering statements, disempowering statements, or even contradictory statements. That's okay. Just let it all come out.

❑ Once complete, look at the statements. Examine the disempowering ones, and consider where you may have picked up that truth about yourself along the way in life. What happened earlier in life, especially in childhood, relating to those you loved and craved love from the most? How did events strengthen those disempowering truths later in life? Then, look at the empowering statements. Think about the events that led to those truths. How and why did you develop those truths about yourself? Who did you want to be like, or who did you not want to be like that led to these empowering truths about yourself? Give yourself some time to reflect deeply on this.

❑ Think about what you are great at, w-ell-known, and loved for. How did those superpowers form within you? Write down any revelations or ah-ha moments you experienced while doing this exercise.

These and all the Action Items from this chapter are included as a checklist in the workbook found on the reader resources page of my website at drkarthikramanan.com/reader-resources

Eat More Fiber

Did you know that 90% of the neurotransmitters that regulate how we think, act, and feel are made by the bacteria that live in our gut? Compounds like serotonin, dopamine, and GABA are vital to nervous system function, and we outsourced that work to these bacteria long ago! We give them a place to live, and they help us with vital life functions like emotional health, immune function, hormone balance, and metabolic function.

We refer to the genetic material contained in these bacteria as the gut microbiome. When we take care of our gut, the bacteria and our gut microbiome take care of us. When we eat processed foods, refined sugars, refined oils, processed meats, and other highly manufactured foods, we create a gut microbiome that isn't in line with how our microbiome might look in nature. Because it's as diverse and unique to us as our fingerprint, there is no "perfect" microbiome; however, an "unnatural" microbiome can't support us in optimal health.

Nutrition science is incredibly vast and highly contested. I'd rank the debates up there with politics: it's hard for people to change their minds, regardless of their beliefs. And perhaps with nutrition, it's even more personal because "you are what you eat" is true! The foods we consume make the building blocks of every cell in our bodies.

In my Good Mood Plant Food course, we delve into this topic in much more detail, but I'll give you the shortcut: eat more fiber!

You can download my Dr. K: Emotional Health Mentor app or visit my website: drkarthikramanan.com to enroll in the Insiders Club and access this (or any of my courses).

When I say, "Eat more fiber," I don't mean a fiber supplement that you mix up in water. I mean fiber from real, actual plants. You know, the ones you get from the produce section of the supermarket or your local farmers' market.

The Recommended Dietary Allowance or adequate fiber intake varies by age and gender, but generally, it is 25 grams per day for women and 38 grams per day for men, or about 14 grams per 1000 calories. Unfortunately, only 5% of Americans get that amount, with the majority taking in just 10-15 grams daily.

Yet, if we look at paleolithic poop studies (yes, there is such a thing), we find that our ancestors ate 100 to 200 grams of fiber per day. Well, that was our ancestors, not us, right? The Hadza tribe of Tanzania presently eats 100 grams per day!

I'm not suggesting you drastically increase your fiber intake that quickly. Your gut wouldn't be able to handle it. It's like strength or endurance training. You don't just go for your goal; you work your way up.

If you want to dive deeply into nutritional science, a book I can't recommend enough is Fiber Fueled by Dr. Will Bulscewicz (2020). I have provided a link on the resources pages of my website if you would like to read that next.

Increasing your fiber intake and eating more whole plants may not immediately improve your emotional health, but you will notice the difference over time.

Good Mood Plant Food Action Items - *Pillars in Practice:*
❑ Look up recipes online for whole food plant-based dishes. Lean towards ones that are less processed. You can find my recommended cookbooks on the reader resources page of my website.
❑ Prepare one whole plant recipe for yourself this week. Take a picture of it on Instagram and tag me at @dr.karthikramanan

These and all the Action Items from this chapter are included as a checklist in the workbook found on the reader resources page of my website at drkarthikramanan.com/reader-resources

20 Minutes of Sun
This one is self-explanatory. We were made for nature, and nature

takes place outside. Nowadays, we get far less sunlight exposure than our ancestors did, and sunlight plays a vital role in our vitality.

Sunlight is critical for vitamin D production, which plays crucial roles in immune function, cardiovascular health, bone health, and brain function. It also helps normalize circadian rhythm, or your body clock, to allow for better sleep at night. Sunlight increases serotonin and endorphin production, which enables us to feel better, regulate stress, and avoid symptoms of depression and seasonal affective disorder. The list goes on.

Strive to get at least 20 minutes of sunlight exposure per day, especially in the morning. If you can add sunlight to your morning routine while doing something else, like journaling or walking, it will amplify the effect of your morning routine and its impact on your emotional health.

Sunlight Action Item - *Pillars in Practice:*
- ❑ Spend 20 minutes outside at least three times over the next week. Notice how you feel in the moment and afterward.

These and all the Action Items from this chapter are included as a checklist in the workbook found on the reader resources page of my website at drkarthikramanan.com/reader-resources

Design Your Ideal Self
When I was leaving my Wall Street career in New York to attend medical school in Arizona, I found myself sitting on the plane at Newark airport in a window seat, literally watching my old life fly away from me. It hit me at that moment that, other than my sister, nobody in Arizona knew me. If there was ever a time to re-invent who I was, that was the moment. I had a spark of inspiration that changed my life, and I'm excited to share it with you.

I took out a sheet of paper and started writing down what this "Dr. K of the future" was like. What are his habits and routines? Who does he spend time with? Who does he not spend time with? What does he eat and not eat? How does he move his body? What does he read? Which podcasts and books does he consume?

I painstakingly outlined this ideal version of myself, and as soon as I landed in Arizona that April day, I used it as a blueprint for how to live my life.

I never saw myself as a leader. I wasn't in high-ranking leadership positions in high school, college, or even my corporate career. (Okay, that's not entirely true. I was president of the chess club in high school for one year because I was the only upperclassman in the club.) I never allowed myself to be a leader because I never saw myself as one.

But what kind of leader would this "Dr. K of the future" be? Well, if I looked at Dr. K's resume, he clearly would have been President of the medical college's Student Government Association, right? Of course he would! So, I joined student government, and in my second year, I ran for President and won. I was scared beyond anything I could describe. It was uncomfortable being responsible for hundreds of fellow students. As we all spent countless hours in classes, clinical settings, and studying for major exams, I had an additional full-time job as president. It was emotionally challenging. I even had my moments of breakdown. But I knew it was what I had to do to become who I wanted to be. Looking back, I'm grateful for my past self's choices.

This is the framework I use to this day to continue to step into my ideal self and push the limits of my comfort zone. Frankly, even writing this book has been one of those actions outside my comfort zone!

By designing your ideal self, you create a vision of the person you want to be. In doing so, you can make each decision on purpose. Do you want to live a reflection of your past, or do you want to live in the vision of who you want to be in the future? Now it's your turn.

Design Your Ideal Self Action Items - *Pillars in Practice:*
- ❑ Set aside 10-15 minutes. Take out a sheet of paper. Describe every detail of the ideal version of yourself.
  - ❑ What language do you use to talk to yourself? What language do you never use towards yourself?
  - ❑ What does your morning routine look like?
  - ❑ What relationship does your ideal self have with your past self?
  - ❑ What do your relationships look like, and who do you spend time with? Who have you forgiven?
  - ❑ How do you eat?
  - ❑ How do you sleep?
  - ❑ How do you move your body?
  - ❑ Which books do you read?
  - ❑ How do you continue to push yourself out of your comfort zone?
  - ❑ How committed are you to growth?
  - ❑ How do you want to make the world around you better?

The workbook includes a checklist of these and all the Action Items from this chapter are included as a checklist in the workbook found on the reader resources page of my website at drkarthikramanan. com/reader-resources

CHAPTER 12

The Emotionally Healthy You

24 Principles for an Emotionally Healthy Life

1. You are not broken.
After struggling long enough, it's easy to think we're broken. Once we feel this way, we unconsciously seek evidence to confirm it. But what if you weren't broken? What if everything could be figured out? What if it just took a different approach and people around you who believe in your ideal self?

2. Your future does not have to be a reflection of your past.
The past can teach us great lessons and only exists in our memories. All we have is the present moment and the choice we need to make right now. That choice can align with who we were or be a step towards the person we want to become.

3. You are not your thoughts or your feelings. Define your true self.
The most accurate freedom comes from defining who we are outside our thoughts, feelings, and circumstances. What if you were the observer of your thoughts, not your thoughts themselves? What if you were the witness to your feelings, not the feelings themselves? What if you are far more than the titles and names you have at this point in life? You are.

4. Remove the obstacles and simplify.
Solving our complex lives doesn't have to be complicated. The

plan is simple. The journey, however, is not easy. We can make it easier by removing the obstacles in our path, even the small ones that add up, and simplifying our lives.

5. Do the things that make you feel alive.
Never forget those activities, hobbies, and interests that make you feel alive and that make you feel most like you. Even as adults, we desire to play. Lean into it, as the smile you develop can carry you through solving other challenges in life.

6. Take back control of your morning.
Technology allows us to do things we never dreamed possible, even not so long ago in human history. However, it also invades our connection to ourselves each day. Leave the phone aside for the first 30 minutes of your day and start your morning on your terms with a routine that inspires you.

7. Commit Yourself to the Relationship (over making yourself right).
When in an argument, it's easy to want to prove yourself right. We might win the argument, but in the long run, we may lose trust and connection with the other person. Instead, ask yourself, "Am I more committed to this relationship, or am I more committed to feeling right?"

8. Eat more fiber.
Your emotional health depends on your gut health, and your gut health depends upon your emotional health. They go hand in hand. Feed your gut bacteria the necessary foods to provide the vital compounds you need—shop in the produce section rather than the aisles. Play with your recipes and have fun exploring!

9. Be a 5-Percenter - A Growth-Seeker.

95% of people are past protectors. And they're not wrong or bad for it; it's how they're wired. They're more committed to upholding the truths they've formed in their lives than they are willing to step outside their comfort zone to live in growth. Anyone can become a Growth Seeker at any point in life. We generally do so once there becomes a need. And once we're a Growth Seeker, there's no turning back. Enjoy the ride!

10. Content, never satisfied.

Often, when we're in the mentality of moving up, whether it's promotions at work or the size of our business as entrepreneurs, it's easy to get caught up in the idea, "When I get there, then I'll be happy." That is until you realize that day never comes. Finding joy is something we can do at any moment. Finding gratitude and peace for being right here, right now, is independent of any future achievement. And we can concurrently be unsatisfied with this moment. When a core purpose for our lives drives us, we know there's no settling. We're on a mission because we know what we are on Earth to do. We can be content in this beautiful moment yet never satisfied with our ability to positively impact people around us.

11. Seek your purpose, then live in it.

Finding our purpose is not a cookie-cutter formula. Life unfolds mysteriously and uniquely for each of us. Everyone's journey is different. Find your purpose by exploring different interests and seeing what sticks. Learn from the pain in your life, and commit yourself to serving others so they may learn from your experiences. Once you find it, let it be the cornerstone purpose of everything you do.

12. Sleep is necessary for emotional resilience.

Sacrificing sleep is not a winning strategy. You don't get a medal in life for burning yourself out. Work hard, and rest fully. We make the best decisions when we are in an emotionally healthy place, and resilience is key. Let your sleep be your recharge.

13. Move your body, especially when you don't want to.

Of the Five Pillars of Emotional Health, body movement can lead to the quickest emotional turnaround. Stretching, walking, running, lifting, breathing, dancing, and playing are all simple means of shifting our emotional state. These bodies are a biological miracle, and moving them allows us to feel connected with ourselves. Do what works for you.

14. Distinguish facts from feelings. Your feelings are valid; they are not always accurate.

It's easy to treat our feelings as facts. Sometimes, they might be, but more often, they are subjective realities. Zoom out, consider what is feeling and what is fact, and choose what you want to focus on. You can also ask yourself, "How do I feel? "How do I want to feel?"

15. When in doubt, ask what your ideal self would do.

Go ahead. Ask yourself, "What would my ideal future self do in this situation?" You can handle it how you want to or how you might have always done it. But what would your future ideal self do in this situation? Do that instead.

16. Become comfortable with discomfort.

Growth is a vital human need that does not come without discomfort. Difficult situations happen in life even when we are emotionally healthy; these experiences become great lessons. If we can redefine our relationship with discomfort, we can grow, make a difference, and stay resilient to life's continuous challenges.

17. Use the power of visualization.
Our memories are powerful. Using visualization, create "memories" of the future, of your ideal self living a deeply meaningful life. Let those memories guide your brain into stepping into that reality.

18. Become ruthlessly selective when designing your environment.
Our environments shape our actions. If you want a ball to roll and you want to expend the least amount of energy, you place it on a declining surface and do little work instead of laying it on a flat or inclining surface and pushing. Our physical, social, and electronic environments drive our life experiences. Become ruthlessly selective in designing your environment, crafting your physical and electronic spaces so it's easier to make choices in line with your ideal self. Surround yourself with people who see you for who you can be. For those with whom you are connected in life, no matter what (like perhaps some family members), show up to those relationships as your ideal self. Let your environment move you toward the person you want to be.

19. Lower your expectations. Raise your standards.
Expectations drive how we feel in response to a situation, and these situations are largely outside our control. Standards dictate what we will and will not tolerate going forward. These are within our control. Focus on the standards. Actions and intentions you can control; their results you cannot choose. So lower your expectations and raise your standards.

20. We change when it hurts enough. Don't wait until it hurts enough.

Biological systems are meant to maintain homeostasis, a sense of active balance, give and take, push and pull. Driving out of homeostasis into a new state of balance is not inherently what any biological system wants to do. But we have the capacity to do so, and we usually change only when it hurts enough. But why wait for life to hurt so much that you make a change? Become your ideal self one moment at a time.

21. Pain happens. Suffering is optional.

Emotional health is not about being impervious to pain. It's about reducing the severity and duration of processing the pain. When we go through a tough situation, it can take as long as it takes to process. There is no perfect timeline. But at some point, we know inside when we've moved from processing to suffering. Life is going to be painful. There are going to be challenges. It's not if, it's when. But we don't need to let it hurt any more than it has to.

22. Never let your pain go to waste. What is this situation allowing you to do?

Pain is our greatest teacher. We learn and grow more from painful situations, losses, and tragedies than we do from our victories. Once we process the situation, how can we learn from this moment and make it count? Ask yourself: what is this situation allowing you to do that you would not be able to do otherwise?

23. Live vicariously through your ideal self.

We can live in the reflection of our pasts. We can live in the circumstances of our present. Or we can live in the vision of our ideal self in the future. Who is the greatest version of you?

Every action you take, every thought you think, every piece of food you place in your mouth, every conversation you have, and every movement you make is simply a vote for the person you want to be. We either move closer to our ideal selves or further away in each moment. So, live vicariously through your ideal self.

24. Stop chasing joy. Begin living in wonder.
As young children, everything is possible. We have no constraints over who we can be or what we can do. We are inherently joyful and need no reason to be; we just are. As we age, we develop guardrails due to messaging from the world around us. We place rules on ourselves for who we think we're expected to be. We chase the next milestone, the next goal, and the next moment as the ones that will yield happiness.

Instead, tap into the childlike wonder inherent in all of us. Who can you become? Surround yourself with people who live in wonder, believe in you, and walk the path of their own purpose. Therein lies inner peace. Therein lies joy.

Stop chasing joy. Begin living in wonder.

I believe in your greatness!

APPENDIX

1. Raichle, Marcus E., and Debra A. Gusnard. "Appraising the Brain's Energy Budget." *Proceedings of the National Academy of Sciences*, vol. 98, no. 2, 2001, pp. 10237-10239, doi: 10.1073/pnas.171643298.

2. Vatansever, et al. "Default Mode Contributions to Automated Information Processing." *Proceedings of the National Academy of Sciences*, vol. 114, no. 30, 2017, pp. 7844-7849, doi: 10.1073/pnas.1710521114.

3. Malik, F., and R. Marwaha. "Cognitive Development." *StatPearls*, updated 23 Apr. 2023, doi: 10.1002/9781118829416.ch2.

4. Korkmaz, Baris. "Theory of Mind and Neurodevelopmental Disorders of Childhood." *Nature Reviews Neurology*, vol. 9, no. 7, 2013, pp. 379-390, doi: 10.1038/nrneurol.2013.111.

5. Tooley, et al. "The Age of Reason: Functional Brain Network Development during Childhood." *Journal of Neuroscience*, vol. 42, no. 44, 2022, pp. 8237-8245, doi: 10.1523/JNEUROSCI.1044-22.2022.

6. Bhattacharya, et al. "Stress Across Generations: DNA Methylation as a Potential Mechanism Underlying Intergenerational Effects of Stress in Both Post-traumatic Stress Disorder and Pre-clinical Predator Stress Rodent Models."

Frontiers in Behavioral Neuroscience, vol. 13, 2019, doi: 10.3389/fnbeh.2019.00113.

7. Schacter, et al. "The Future of Memory: Remembering, Imagining, and the Brain." *Neuron*, vol. 76, no. 4, 2012, pp. 677-694, doi: 10.1016/j.neuron.2012.11.001.

8. Freud, Sigmund. *The Interpretation of Dreams*. Translated by A. A. Brill, Macmillan, 1913.

9. Clance, Pauline Rose, and Suzanne Ament Imes. "The Imposter Phenomenon in High Achieving Women: Dynamics and Therapeutic Intervention." *Psychotherapy: Theory, Research and Practice*, vol. 15, no. 3, 1978, pp. 241-247.

10. Goleman, Daniel. *Emotional Intelligence: Why It Can Matter More Than IQ*. Bantam Books, 1995.

11. Gringras, et al. "Bigger, Brighter, Bluer-Better? Current Light-Emitting Devices - Adverse Sleep Properties and Preventative Strategies." *Sleep Health*, vol. 1, no. 4, 2015, pp. 311-318, doi: 10.1016/j.sleh.2015.06.002.

12. Ricketts, et al. "Electric Lighting, Adolescent Sleep and Circadian Outcomes, and Recommendations for Improving Light Health." *Sleep Health*, vol. 7, no. 3, 2021, pp. 257-265, doi: 10.1016/j.sleh.2021.02.002.

13. Francavilla, et al. "Regulation of Neurotransmitters by the Gut Microbiota and Effects on Cognition in Neurological Disorders." *Frontiers in Cellular Neuroscience*, vol. 16, 2022, doi: 10.3389/fncel.2022.8234057.

14. Barandouzi, et al. "Associations of Neurotransmitters and the Gut Microbiome with Emotional Distress in Mixed Type of Irritable Bowel Syndrome." *Scientific Reports*, vol. 12, no. 1, 2022, doi: 10.1038/s41598-022-05756-0.

15. Braga, et al. "Gamma-aminobutyric Acid as a Potential Postbiotic Mediator in the Gut–Brain Axis." *Nature Communications*, vol. 15, no. 1, 2024, doi: 10.1038/s41467-024-49253-2.

16. Borrego-Ruiz, et al. "Human Gut Microbiome, Diet, and Mental Disorders." *Nutrients*, vol. 16, no. 10, 2024, doi: 10.1007/s10123-024-00518-6.

17. Asnicar, et al. "Microbiome Connections with Host Metabolism and Habitual Diet from 1,098 Deeply Phenotyped Individuals." *Nature Communications*, vol. 12, no. 1, 2021, doi: 10.1038/s41467-021-23597-7.

18. Saghafian, et al. "Consumption of Dietary Fiber in Relation to Psychological Disorders in Adults." *Nutrients*, vol. 13, no. 11, 2021, doi: 10.3390/nu13113841.

19. Quagliani, et al. "Closing America's Fiber Intake Gap." *Nutrition Today*, vol. 53, no. 3, 2018, pp. 129-142, doi: 10.1097/NT.0000000000000286.

20. Eaton, et al. "The Ancestral Human Diet: What Was It and Should It Be a Paradigm for Contemporary Nutrition?" *American Journal of Clinical Nutrition*, vol. 72, no. 3, 2000, pp. 691-703, doi: 10.1093/ajcn/72.3.691.

21. Goldman, Bruce. "Hunter-Gatherers of Tanzania Experience Seasonal Variation in Gut-Microbe Diversity." *Stanford Medicine News Center*, 2017.

ACKNOWLEDGMENTS

To my parents, Aruna and Sri. Thank you for all the courageous sacrifices you made to allow me to live the life I lead today.

To my sister, Sulinya. Your guidance and wisdom during my life's most pivotal moments are gifts for which I can never adequately thank you.

To my wife, Samantha. I could not ask for a better person to have beside me in this life. Together, we amplify each others' dreams, living not in circumstance but in the possibility of who we can become and how greatly we can serve others. You reminded me from the start that to change the world, we will inherently not fit in. Thank you for your unconditional love. Thank you for believing in my greatness.

www.ingramcontent.com/pod-product-compliance
Lightning Source LLC
Chambersburg PA
CBHW061809120626
46550CB00005B/2197